THE PASTOR AS THEOLOGIAN

New Library of Pastoral Care

The Pastor as Theologian

*The formation of today's
ministry in the light of
contemporary human sciences*

Second edition

Wesley Carr

To Natalie

First published in Great Britain in 1989

Society for Promoting Christian Knowledge
36 Causton Street
London SW1P 4ST

Reprinted once
Second edition published 2008

British Library Cataloguing-in-Publication Data
A catalogue record for this book is available from the British Library

ISBN 978–0–281–06037–5

1 3 5 7 9 10 8 6 4 2

Typeset by Kenneth Burnley
Printed in Great Britain by Ashford Colour Press

Produced on paper from sustainable forests

Contents

Acknowledgements

The fundamental work on the revision of *The Pastor as Theologian* was done while I was Erikson Scholar at Austen Riggs Center, Stockbridge, Massachusetts, in 2006. I am grateful to the whole community for the welcome they extended to Natalie and me. Special thanks are due to the CEO and Medical Director, Dr Edward Shapiro, and to Dr Gerard Fromm, Director of the Erikson Institute.

Preface

This is an essay in theology. And like all theology it is written using a model drawn from the contemporary world. Usually theologians take a literary or philosophical perspective; often they write large volumes. I was privileged to go with some colleagues from Graduate School at Geneva to visit Karl Barth. Vatican II had just ended. An earnest young American asked whether this was a new spring in theology. The professor answered drily, 'If it is spring, where are the flowers?' Things have not changed greatly: it is a time when there are many books still being published, but there is no joyful exultation at a new spring. It is more like a British February – a messy winter and a season of the occasional aconite or snowdrop. This is a small contribution to contemporary theological debate as well as pastoral ministry.

It is unusual because it works in the opposite direction from that to which we are accustomed. In spite of the ferment in educational practice and theory, we are still mostly familiar with the idea of first learning some theology and then applying it to a situation or to oneself. It is, for example, endemic in churches that, as soon as a new initiative for lay activity is produced, the first request will be for more training. We seem to think that only when we have enough knowledge can we be fit for action. And, of course, we never acquire enough. The pastor has similar feelings. The difference is that he or she (as public representatives of the Church – and even God) is expected to know already. People, both within the Church and outside, look to a publicly authorized person for answers. If pastors are not theologians, then they cannot respond; and if they cannot interpret their people's approach, then they fail as pastors. And if they cannot hold the two – theology and pastoral ministry – these may combine to undermine the pastor's own faith.

A way of integrating theology, pastoral activity and personal faith is essential. For this purpose the theologian is the pastor. His or her world is dominated by action which may lead to reflection and in some instances to theological reflection. Today theology, as with so many other disciplines, is more complex and more contentious than for many a year. This is partly because of the variety of contexts in which we are set and partly as a result of the widespread loss of a sense of personal responsibility, especially for roles that are ours and that, as they say, 'go with the territory'.

One effect of these changes is the way in which the term 'theological reflection' has emerged. It appeared about twenty years ago and to an extent replaced the then dominant theme of 'doing theology'. One problem with each of these was that students were unclear about what was expected of them, and their teachers were not too sure themselves.

It is, therefore, not surprising that a recent book on the subject is explicitly directed at professors and senior students.[1] The authors rightly and cogently argue that 'practical theology should have the status of a primary theological discipline because of its roots in concrete human dilemmas'. That is very like the position from which this book is written. These authors' characterization of theological reflection, had it prevailed throughout the life of the Church, has five foci. There would not be much disagreement about these, bearing in mind that they are hypothetical. Theological enquiry would arise from human dilemmas and contexts; theological formulations would be generated from the creative use of inherited and contemporary concepts; 'talk about God' would be seen to be a human activity; theology would be practical wisdom; the practice of theology would be a disciplined reflection on how talk of God emerges from human experience and questions.

This is not what has happened, nor should we expect it to become the mark of the churches. For books on pastoral studies and theological reflection usually, if not always, seem to lose the messiness of human interactions. We misunderstand one another; we fail to see alternatives to positions that we hold; especially, so it seems, in the Church we confuse authority with power. Yet these are all issues that particularly affect (and are affected by) pastoral activity and theological reflection. In this book I have tried to address some of these.

GROUPS AND GROUP RELATIONS

Alongside my work in the Church, I have sustained for many years an interest in the study of groups. Since few of my colleagues and friends are either Christian or religious, I have had the benefit of having many opportunities in an astringent but holding environment to rethink my personal faith and my formal role as a priest. But it was a while before I saw an obvious connection. The study of groups, as offered by the Tavistock Institute of Human Relations, works with a fundamental theory that there are three psychological stances that a group may adopt. It also happens that each of these three is fundamental to one primary Christian doctrine. With hindsight it should not have been a surprise to find they each relate in this fashion. For things human must be prominent in any theology that interprets the story of Bethlehem as incarnation, Golgotha as atonement, and the garden sepulchre as new creation.

The other point that these connections indicate is that both for acknowledging God and for preaching the gospel, we need a theological stance that today takes into account what we have learned about what it means to be human. The behavioural sciences cannot be ignored. They have in the last two hundred years moved from the periphery of medicine to being a major contributor to neurology and other social studies. They, too, must therefore influence theological thinking at least as much as they have impacted on pastoral activity.

'Pastoral', too, remains something of an enigma. We all reckon to know what it means until we have to define it. It then may turn out to be (in Peter Hebblethwaite's term) 'broken backed'.[2] This was after a mauling it received among the cardinals when they had to elect a new pope after the sudden demise of John Paul I. All, whatever his role had been, claimed to be pastoral.

Wherever we turn today, therefore, whether to our theology (thinking about God), to our pastoring (representing God) or to our personal journey of faith (exploring the spiritual life), the behavioural sciences need to be taken into account.

CHANGES IN THE NEW EDITION

The original edition of *The Pastor as Theologian* is now out of print. Yet it remains one of my books about which people still ask

me questions. It is as if they appreciate the value of the interpretations of ministry which are offered, but cannot quite grasp the
psychological theory in the early part of the book. I, too, have felt
uncomfortable with just reproducing the original. There are as a
result two main differences in the revision.

The first is a reduction of the theoretical part in order to reach
the overtly theological material more quickly. This book is offered
as a contribution to theology. It is not just about pastoral activity.
In the first edition I followed a 'traditional' order: setting out the
issues; offering a theory and then applying it. But it was clear
that readers were skimming or ignoring the theory. They recognized that it was important, but on the whole wished to pursue it
in less intense fashion. And, of course, they were right: the theme
of the book is the way that the practice of ministry generates
theological insight. The pastor's practice informs (as well as being
informed by) theological reflection. In this regard much of the
material on the role of the pastor as teacher and the connexion of
belief in God with transitional objects has been dispersed. It
comes up in the course of the discussion, but I felt that beginning
with it became a barrier rather than help.

The second major change is the order in which the doctrines
are discussed. We still take three Christian 'classics' – atonement
(crucifixion), creation/resurrection and incarnation. This is
purely practical; there is no question that the doctrine of the
incarnation, and the relevant human sciences, is the most difficult of the three. It is not, therefore, the best starting point. By
changing the order of consideration the book becomes easier to
read without losing the basic thrust. (See the table on p. xi for a
schematic view of the argument.)

There are three major doctrines (left hand column). Each holds
a basic psychological dynamic that may be discerned in it (right
hand column). These are known as 'basic assumptions' and are
discussed in the first chapter. Within that nexus are found both
the individual and the corporate aspects to the pastor's life – her
ministry (second column from the left) and her personal discipleship (third column). The aim is to indicate how these might be
integrated in today's pastor.

There remain acknowledgements, but after a lifetime of public
ministry the sources blur. So this comes with gratitude to many,
especially faithful and holy women and men whom it has been
my privilege to know. One person, however, made a distinctive

Doctrine	Pastoral ministry	Discipleship	Dynamic
Atonement	Handling projection	Spirituality	Fight/flight
Creation/ resurrection	Ritual	Worship	Dependence
Incarnation	Using differences	Prayer	Pairing

contribution to this edition. Recently a friend and colleague of many years' standing, Canon Frank Telfer, reread it and then willingly read much of the redraft. His insightful comments have proved immensely valuable and contribute much to this new edition. For SPCK, Ruth McCurry has been a supportive and loyal editor. The dedicatee remains loved and admired by many, especially me.

Wesley Carr
November 2007

Note

The New Dictionary of Pastoral Studies (SPCK, 2002) has been published since the first edition. It was designed precisely for readers of this type of book. There are no references to it; but I assume that the reader has it beside him or her.

The term 'pastor' is used, as in the original, interchangeably with 'minister'; and 'he' and 'she' are deployed in an inclusive sense, unless the context indicates otherwise.

The inadvertent chaplain

Westminster Abbey is a unique institution. In 2006 I resigned as Dean of Westminster because of ill health. And another unique institution beckoned: I was invited to become for six months the Erikson Scholar at Austen Riggs Center in Stockbridge, Massachusetts. This is the last purely psychoanalytically based clinic in the United States – a remarkable thing in itself, given the intellectual and social investment in psychotherapy, and particularly psychoanalysis, that characterized the USA in the earlier part of the twentieth century. As the CEO and Medical Director put it, 'We bother with those who bother us.' The patients are often at their wits' end, having been treated by many psychiatrists and doctors without success. Briefly, at Riggs the patients live in an open setting. They are known by the people of the town. The treatment consists of an integrated programme of individual psychotherapy along with community and group activities. I have had an association with the clinic and its director, Dr Edward Shapiro, a colleague and friend, over many years. The invitation, therefore, was both welcome and warming.

The Scholar is expected to contribute to the life of the community, to research, to do some teaching and to write. So for six months my wife and I lived as members of this community. Austen Riggs, like any modern clinical institution, works on the basis of methodological atheism. Belief in a God is not required nor is it denied. But like most contemporary secular organizations, it has relegated religion largely to being a private matter. To have, therefore, an English Anglican priest, particularly one with a high public profile, resident among them was for all of us a learning experience. Within hours of my arrival in my office one of the therapists called to ask if I could tell her why she was so disliked. I had, of course, no idea, but agreed to talk about it later.

The second visitor began with the question 'Do you do God?' to which I replied nothing was out of bounds. Gradually, however, the place settled down to my presence and I was asked from time to time my views on religious matters but also occasionally on psychological issues and indeed the course of treatment which people were receiving.

Several specifically religious issues arose, two of which are outlined here. About 18 months prior to our arrival, a distinguished and much loved member of the staff had died. His funeral had been held; a memorial event was in mind, but the real problem was that people did not know what to do about the burial. They could not put a closure on ending; the ultimate separation was not being faced. The staff member in charge had a word with me; someone had reminded him that I had some experience of funerals. He talked about 'dedicating' a gravestone in the town cemetery. I pointed out that on the whole one did not dedicate or unveil gravestones: they were just there. But something was needed. The deceased had had a way of using catchphrases. Two came from the Bible – 'I will lift up my eyes to the hills' (from Psalm 121) and 'Don't fret' (from Philippians 4.6). When we examined these, things became clear and people realized that they had the basis of a simple service of memorial and suitable inscriptions for the headstone. I was asked to draft the service and I was willing to do so, since it mobilized a skill that was not prominent in that environment. We had a short but moving ceremony round the headstone in the cemetery before returning to the main house for remembrances and refreshment.

The second story is of a particularly sad event – the suicide of a young patient. Fortunately these are rare. The whole clinic was shocked by this event and I was approached by one or two people in order to discuss what it was doing to them. The staff in charge of the patients, and some patients themselves, asked me if I would meet with as many patients as wished in order to discuss this tragic event. I agreed to do so and, with the director present, met about 30 patients for an hour's discussion. I did not say much other than to introduce the afternoon. I then fielded a range of questions to do with suicide, death, the Church, religion, and all the other aspects of life which had been disturbed by this tragedy.

One of the most interesting, and I think unforeseen, outcomes occurred after this session. The therapists found that their patients talked about the religious dimension to life, an exploration which hitherto had not on the whole arisen. In spite of the excellent treatment and widely recognized (and achieved) aims of the clinic, there was an area of people's lives which they did not customarily explore but which, when it was exposed, had for many a significant impact upon their lifestyle and life programme.

It is as if I became an unofficial chaplain to the institution, not to the staff or the patients particularly, but to the institution as a whole. In that role I carried the dependence of the patients on a different bandwidth from that which they normally used with the therapists. I certainly did not offer treatment. Nevertheless my presence indicated and allowed exploration, albeit briefly, of another boundary, that ultimately between heaven and hell, life and death, God and man, and so on.

The role of a chaplain has been described as 'to loiter with intent' and this is one way in which the institution can work out issues of dependency. But without the catalyst of a representative of transcendence (this need not necessarily be a priest, although it does seem to help if the person concerned is obviously authorized), it seems that a dimension of life can remain unexplored. It will certainly do this through an unconscious collusion of the therapist and patient, both being modern secular people and committed to methodological atheism. It may be that this could be intellectually value neutral; but in practice it cannot be. For this mediating presence is a means by which a society carries its values. And in the West the Church has been, and seems often to remain, 'chaplain to society'.

It is for such a task that theological reflection is essential. But for the Christian that reflection will be informed by the context as much as by the tradition and Scripture. It is to that task we now turn.

CHAPTER ONE

Introduction

THE HUMAN SCIENCES

Pastoring is a human activity. It requires people, often in depth or unexpected intimacy, to engage with one another, whether as individuals or as groups. The pastor is at home as much in a sick visit as, say, a youth club. Such variety may be stimulating but it can also be debilitating. One major reason for that is that we usually have too little grasp of the human dynamics that are being generated. We feel that we may have done a course and recognize that there are these dynamics, but we do not have the tools to understand them, let alone use them. Such ministry, therefore, needs to develop a way of holding together the pastor's personal life and his or her roles. We hear much about person and role with regard to ministry, and the minister's personal faith both affects and is affected by moments of ministry. What is more, faith (one's own) and faith (one's public role) intertwine and are frequently called upon. There is, therefore, all the more reason to attempt some clarity, so that the ministry may become more effective and the minister not be exhausted. In the pastoral encounter, the gospel that motivates the minister and the reality of whatever in their life is driving those asking for pastoral intervention come together. And whatever the theological differences, an integrating model would reflect a basic agreement on what it is to be human.

During their modern development, pastoral studies have been increasingly associated with the 'human', or 'behavioural', sciences, that had such an impact on the twentieth century. These disciplines earned their name 'human' in the late nineteenth and early twentieth centuries. The new approach, as represented for example by Sigmund Freud, was premised on the basis that the structures of our internal world could be discernible. This discovery was important for both the individual and society. Things that were not customarily addressed were opened up. For example, dreams have been prominent in many societies. But Freud first proposed a coherent and ordering way of interpreting them. This is not to discount prophets and seers of all times; but the new psycho-analysis gave dreams a continuing place in the modern world. And as technology advanced, for all the questions that it raised, the 'talking cure' has preserved within psychiatry the central concept of 'human'. In the face of fast emerging psycho-pharmacology, for instance, it has sustained the humanness of talking. In very broad terms let us see what is in the field.

Psychology

Psychology, and the psychology of religion in particular, has tended to be preoccupied with the individual. It has not ignored social dimensions in society or failed to acknowledge groups. Yet it always seems, when pressured, to lean towards the individual. The pastor, however, while not ignoring or discounting the individual, will, in principle and often in practice, come from the opposite direction, from the group to the individual. He or she has many roles and social functions, and for these to work groups are critical. This issue is extensively explored in this book. In our pastoral studies we need to bring together these issues and the Christian tradition, as well as the current experience of the Church's members.

Sociology

This discipline has many historic links with religion, for it was in that field that much early sociology was developed. But some church people became frightened. It seemed to claim to determine the behaviour of individuals and societies, thus removing individual autonomy, or, at least, responsibility. Thus it was one of the main studies that was believed to undermine faith, more so than psychology. At one modern university the divinity professor was daily annoyed by the fact that the 'godless' sociologists occupied the floor above. Their place should have been in the basement.

But churches encompass the whole world in their vision and much religious experience occurs with others in groups. There cannot be pastoral studies without sociology. Anthropology also has something to offer, but not as clearly as psychology and sociology.

Psychoanalysis

There is one other important discipline – depth psychology or psychoanalysis. From its earliest days in the late nineteenth century, this has had a mixed reception. On the one hand it came so to dominate the thinking of some, that it was suggested that if everyone was analysed the world would be a better place. It was, of course, an analyst who said so. On the other hand its insights were of continuing significance. They attracted artists, especially novelists and playwrights.

At first it was for the individual, almost totally avoiding context. It saw people in terms of drives within. Subsequently the notion of object relations emerged. This, as the name suggests, thought of development in terms of relationships. Later, however, the study of group behaviour used it as one resource, but not the only one, in developing a model with which to explore how people behave with one another and why.

> [The individual] uses [others] and they him, to express views, to take action, and play roles. The individual is a creature of a group, the group of the individual.[1]

This is the approach adopted as the co-ordinating behavioural model alongside theological themes in this book. It is this bringing together individual and group on a shared psychological and theological base that I am attempting to create and inviting pastors to join.

By the end of the twentieth century behavioural studies (or human sciences) were recognized both theoretically and as making a contribution to neurological science, and practically by their employment in therapy and consultancy. What is more, they have opened to us aspects of the human which are critical for theologians. In particular, they provide us with a structure on which we can bring together the gospel as we believe it, the Church's life (primarily of prayer and worship), and the life of members of the human race to whom we minister. The thrust of this book is that it is by practice that we shall learn, and that therefore the theory follows and interprets experience.

OSKAR PFISTER

Improbable though it sounds, one of the first to grasp the significance of Freud's discoveries was a Swiss pastor, Oskar Pfister. Today we might be inclined to regard Pfister's interest as a straying from the theological basis of his pastorate. But in context we see how early Freud's thinking affected more than his immediate coterie and the relief it brought to at least one (but undoubtedly more) pastors:

> I tried forthwith to apply these discoveries [Freud's ideas] to my ministry and found to my joy that I could now discover facts and render help in a way that since then has not failed.[2]

The relationship was lifelong, and Pfister did not sell out his religious convictions to these new psychological ones. Quite what one would make of the relationship is not clear, but it is obvious that Freud held this pastor in high regard and the feeling was mutual. There are few pastors who would be so convinced today.

A brief introduction to some of the language used in this field is necessary. Those who are new to such thinking I ask to run with it for the time being and see how it works out before you make your judgement. To those who are familiar with it, you could omit this chapter or, perhaps, read it quickly to check whether you and I are using familiar terms in any unfamiliar fashions.

THE END TO TALKING

There has probably never been another institution in the world that has been so dependent upon words and language as the Church. And equally there has not been an institution so rent by dispute and difference over meanings. The poet Edwin Muir memorably noted of the Scottish chapel, 'the Word made flesh is here made words again'. But this process of wrangling began long before. The disciples disputed as they followed Jesus. It continues in Luke's account of the earliest days in Acts; and remains to this day. Of all people, therefore, Christians should be among the most understanding when they survey the talkative contemporary behavioural sciences.

Freud's 'talking cure' relies upon the most human of activities, talking. But it includes listening in a new way. This is to listen for what is not being said or verbal mistakes, popularly known as a 'Freudian slip'. The social context of this development, together with the characters of those involved and their professional relations, produced difference, dispute and frequently acrimony. The controversy is not over, but through the smoke of discord, we can discern a basic thrust in the discipline.

Three fundamental concepts emerge. A great deal of evidence seems to confirm them and there is now widespread agreement about them. Each is an aspect of our behaviour. Notice I said 'our'. For they are not tools for the expert to diagnose what is wrong with someone or some group. They are also addressed to all participants in any pastoral engagement. The three are: unconscious activity, transference (and its corollary, counter-transference) and projection.

Each is a large concept, but together they provide tools with which systematically to explore our human life and behaviour. Some appreciation of them is essential for any enterprise that involves human encounters, including ours. It is not a matter of surrendering to psychobabble; nor is it an alternative, new gospel. I simply suggest that all of us from time to time long to find a way of thinking that brings together pastoral activity (the outside demand) and our theological knowledge that informs our ministry (the inside uncertainty about the role we are in), and this is for two reasons.

First, there is the matter of feelings being shrouded in talk; as one representing God we need to learn to think with our hearts as well as our minds. And we need, therefore, a way of doing this and a language in which to communicate between us. Second, there is also our personal self, who cannot be ignored. As an American scholar wrote with reference to funerals, however many she has done, 'the minister always grieves too'.

UNCONSCIOUS ACTIVITY

The study of human psychology began long before its modern blossoming. The idea, however, that a dimension of human life that we do not directly experience may be systematically explored underlies much contemporary thought. Controversy about what precisely is being identified and examined continues. But for our purposes it is enough to recognize that there is such an area and that it can be examined. We cannot in our theological thinking retreat from this new terrain, even though it may be unfamiliar.

'Unconscious' may be either a noun or an adjective. Today it is widely and casually used as a noun – 'the unconscious'. It refers to that part deep within where motivations, on which we do not reflect and of which we are scarcely aware, operate. That is why Freud called dreams 'the royal road to the unconscious'. This does not, however, in the light of subsequent developments, imply the idea of something inside us called 'the unconscious'. Rather we are 'people who think, imagine, feel and act, sometimes consciously, sometimes unconsciously'.[3] The contrast is not between conscious and unconscious, the former appearing in the guise of our more rational decisions and the latter emerging as irrational behaviour.

Unconscious activity is as important a factor in our everyday life as conscious reflection. But because unconscious activity is a different sort of process from that of conscious activity, we cannot be aware of all its elements. From time to time, however, some may come to our attention. We may, for example, not follow Freud in his view of dreams. But we all dream and know from that experience that we can be aware of processes within us that relate to who we are. But dream experience is qualitatively different from the tenets by which we deliberately choose to live. Where else do we both observe some drama and play a major role in it, too? It is that area of life, however we interpret it and become aware of its existence, which is called 'unconscious'. Today the idea is so widespread – even though not always understood – that it is difficult, if not impossible, to live in the prevailing intellectual climate, without acknowledging this dimension of our humanity.

One major development already mentioned has been an increasing grasp of the significance of relationships. Donald Winnicott, notable above all for his work with disturbed children, always emphasized that, whenever a child was presented to him, he never saw only a child; there was always the child/mother relationship to consider. This emphasis on relationship reminds us that unconscious processes are not private, arising from within an isolated individual. They are part of the self, which grows from and through relationship with others.

Example: the study group

Eight people in a church study group were discussing the resurrection. They were not finding it easy, as they questioned their beliefs and found passages of the Gospels obscure. The name of

David Jenkins, one-time Bishop of Durham,[4] was introduced, it seemed almost casually. As one, the group began to indulge in anti-intellectual and anti-episcopal argument and cohered. Members appeared to feel better, being let off the hook of their own questions and of having to examine themselves. On another occasion the same group faced another controversial topic. This time they sat around telling stories and exchanging anecdotes; some arrived late; coffee took an interminable time to make and serve; and the evening evaporated in chit-chat.

The way that this group behaved on each occasion illustrates conscious and unconscious behaviour. At a conscious level the members assembled to study and learn; they took that decision and attended. Unconsciously, however, there were other purposes, which emerged in different ways. The unconscious life of the group seems to have been designed to defend the members against learning which might change them and their beliefs. First they attacked a notional enemy, who was not, of course, really opposed to them. They were never likely to be involved directly with the Bishop of Durham, and accordingly he was unreal as someone with whom to engage. On the second occasion they colluded in elevating trivial things and activities so as to allow them to escape the stress of beginning to study. The precise dynamics of this group are unimportant for present purposes; we need simply to note conscious and unconscious behaviour.

Discerning the unconscious is crucial for our estimates of people, both as individuals and in groups. It is a recognized dimension of our human existence, and any gospel for today must include reflection on how God may address us in this facet of ourselves. This is even more necessary when that gospel is proclaimed by men and women who offer a pastoral ministry which is informed by awareness of unconscious influences in human life.

TRANSFERENCE

Most of us have at some time heard a joke about the relationship between a patient and a psychiatrist in which a patient uses the therapist to represent someone or something significant. The joke often revolves around his not representing but actually becoming someone, such as the patient's father. This is transference, and its complement is counter-transference. 'Transference' is occasionally used in a general sense, but on the

whole it remains a technical term for a process by which unconscious wishes are made accessible, so that they can be identified
and interpreted. But the manifestations of transference are not
straightforward repetitions of the past brought into the present
but are instances of unconscious wishes.

How transference functions and how exactly it should be
understood remain disputed. But there is little doubt about the
process itself. It generates a relationship in which feelings (such
as love, hate and resentment) are felt more powerfully than the
actual situation demands. The patient, for example, does not in
'real' terms love or hate the analyst. But in the setting between
them he may experience such emotions. As these are allowed –
even encouraged – and interpreted, hitherto obscure processes
that have underlying influence on a person's life may be revealed
and addressed. In transference, the patient 'transfers' on to the
analyst feelings and attitudes, most likely derived from childhood
relationships.

There are problems with such a notion, but these do not immediately affect the basic insight and its importance for pastoring.
For we are not concerned with the specific content and detail of
transference so much as with the fact of the process itself. This is
not confined to therapy. The concept of transference takes us into
the heart of everyday human life – our relationships with one
another – and consequently into questions about who we ourselves are. It is a central insight for contemporary life, and, as
will appear, for theology and pastoral practice.

One of Freud's early associates, Sandor Ferenczi, soon recognized that this idea had a much wider application, and Freud
himself acknowledged the same point: '[Transference] is a universal phenomenon of the human mind . . . and in fact dominates the
whole of each person's relations to his human environment.'[5] This
is, therefore, a dimension to human life of which the pastor needs
to be aware. It is about using and being used.

COUNTER-TRANSFERENCE

All of us are in some way caught up in this, not least when speaking of 'being used'. For pastors, without the defensive security of a
contract – time, place and payment – the complementary notion
to transference, namely counter-transference, is especially important. This acknowledges the obvious, but frequently overlooked,
fact that any relationship, however professional, is between two

feeling human beings. Therapists have sometimes been pictured as blank screens on which patients draw their own fantasies, or as unresponsive receptacles for whatever the patient may wish to dispose of. Yet these images are clearly deficient. When people meet, whatever the formal structure of their relationship, feelings are to some degree reciprocal.

The term 'counter-transference' describes the feeling response of a person who is the focus for transference. Counter-transference is also universal. Because everyday pastoral encounters are less structured than, for example, a meeting of a doctor with a patient, there is more space for unaddressed transference on the part of the person approaching the minister and for unrecognized counter-transference in return. For the pastor, as will become clear later, awareness of this is especially important. In the informal setting of most of their ministry, it is the means of entry to the dynamic world in which they are working. 'What is happening to me?' is a better ministerial question than 'What is the matter with him?'

Every encounter which we have with individuals or with groups contains this element. If we are aware that people are using us in some fashion, then we need also to be aware that to some extent we too are probably using them. The professional question is how such feelings are recognized, acknowledged, handled and used.

Transference and counter-transference are not remote, theoretical ideas. They describe fundamental human behaviour that occurs both between individuals and within groups. Some grasp of it, therefore, provides a valuable resource in the day-to-day work of ministry. We shall return to this later. And there is also the theological question. When we consider how God engages with our unconscious aspects, we shall have to take into account the process of transference and counter-transference.

PROJECTION

The third key notion is 'projection'. This is also a process with which most of us are familiar, even if the term is not used. Transference involves a repetition of the past by imposing an aspect of that past on something or someone in the present. It also, however, arises spontaneously in human relationships. Projection is similarly a universal phenomenon, but it is a facet of present behaviour. The term describes the way in which we seek to escape from distress by disowning an aspect of ourselves that we wish to deny or refuse to face. We locate it in another person and deal with it there as 'their fault', so freeing ourselves. And for the most part we are unaware of what is happening. As with the other processes, we have learned that projection is not solely an individual form of behaviour. It is also a characteristic of groups. Indeed, as a phenomenon it is sometimes more easily discerned in a group or an organization.

Example: a hospital

When we are surrounded with sickness and death, the complex series of roles that people hold generates powerful but disturbingly intimate emotions. As a result, different groups, which have legitimate functions in the treatment programme, may become identified and used for other covert purposes.

Nurses, for instance, have a vital function along with doctors in providing care and treatment. But doctors may not wish to acknowledge the messiness of patient care, and so leave this to the nurses. This can be claimed to be legitimate; it is 'nurses' work'. But it may also be a way of disowning the mess that is part of the doctors' responsibilities that they do not wish to face. Thus different individuals or groups of people are relied on to hold feelings, which are redistributed within the setting of everyday working. This may relieve one set of people in the organization, but in another group it produces an uncomfortable sense that something is wrong, although people are unsure what.

Example: the verger

Ministers will be familiar with similar phenomena in churches. A verger may seem to be filled with strong feelings, the origins of which he cannot identify and which he can express only in an angry outburst. The reason may be that the minister and/or the congregation are projecting into people, whose views (it is believed) can be disregarded, stresses and feelings that are arising from the church's activities. In ecclesiastical folklore, vergers are often characterized as temperamental and 'difficult' people. When they leave, however, the episode is 'understood' in terms of their personality and presumed inability to get on with others.

This phenomenon of individual and corporate projection has become a more prominent idea as thinking has moved away from an earlier preoccupation with instincts, towards our modern awareness of relationships. All relationships are to some degree projective, and the same dynamic applies to companies and nations. It is often considered something to be discerned and dealt with, so as to help an individual towards maturity, or, in the case of a group or members of an organization, to more purposeful and effective work. This is not a wholly unsound approach, but it is also important to perceive that, like unconscious activity and transference, projection is a basic, or given, form of normal human behaviour. If it is appreciated as such, it can become creative for all concerned.

The pastor who wishes to be effective needs to be alive to projective behaviour. A public role such as his or hers is liable to be a focus for others to project aspects of themselves into him or her. But ministers also need to reflect on what they may inadvertently be projecting into others. Again, as with the other terms that we have examined, ministers also require a theological interpretation of the place of projection in the way God engages with our human life at its unconscious level.

SUMMARY

These three insights – unconscious process, transference and projection – undergird contemporary thinking about human behaviour, both individual and corporate.[6] There is no agreement about the precise interpretation of any of them, yet there is widespread agreement that they are significant. For our purposes, we can now see that, although the field is fraught with problems and disputes, there is no intrinsic hostility between analytically informed thinking, upon which both sophisticated and popular views of contemporary common human experience depend, and theological interpretation. Either religion is concerned with these central aspects of human life and development or it is irrelevant. God, likewise, must be interpretable in some fashion in this specific world. Or if not, the pastor and theologian will eventually lose touch with contemporary men and women.

THE GROUP BEHIND THE GROUP

There is one further point. We always consider the individual in his or her setting. Thus the individual, even when the focus of attention, brings a context with her. This is part of the individual with which she reacts. The pastor therefore needs to be able to recognize the influence of groups in any pastoral situation. The need for holding together the individual and his/her groups (ranging from the family to the nation) can hardly be mentioned without the name of Wilfred Bion.

Bion was one of those people who sees a broader canvas and responds to the challenge of making sense. A noted analyst, he was taking therapy groups when he noticed that there was another level of behaviour going on. As individuals the participants were dealing with their health and welfare. But underneath there were unconscious divisions, disagreements; above all, there was the unspoken rage against him as consultant because of his interpretation of what he thought was happening. There was another 'group' going on, of which the members were unaware because it was unconscious. But it was having an effect on the group as a whole and on the members individually.

Bion, cutting a long history short, discerned three modes of such behaviour which he called 'basic assumptions'. In dependence, people rely upon someone, often the consultant, to rescue them from pain or distress. Pairing is an intensified form of dependence that sets up two people to produce a reliable saviour. And fight/flight is the unstable assumption which sometimes mobilizes action, even though it, too, is a defence against work.

The value of these to the pastor, however, is that, even if he does not grasp what is going on, he will have at his fingertips approaches towards handling the feelings intended for him and so be able to risk interpreting what is going on in the group. The group is not everything, but it is certainly more often where the pastor will start from.

THEOLOGY

Amid these emerging understandings theological education for ordinands has also gone through major change and readjustment. In part that is due to general changes in education policy, but it is also related to the quality of students, their experience in learning and what can be offered on the course to produce a pas-

toral clergy. In the Church of England the proportion of ordinands aged 35 and over has increased. When they talk of the
'University of Life' we know we are in trouble. The colleges and
courses are caught between, on the one hand, the need to fill out
the person's experiences with knowledge – Scripture, liturgy,
history and theology – and on the other the need to prepare them
for roles inside and outside the congregation, thus sending forth
people who can work in and eventually take charge of parishes.

The 'product' should remain the ideal of the learned pastor.
And to the dimensions of learning and pastoring we must add a
third – the pastor's own spiritual life. When a person's self is up
for constant scrutiny, then the stress will affect every part of
them, including their 'private' spiritual life. We can use the model
of testimony. Testimony is the personal witness of a Christian to
his or her faith with his or her own passion. It sometimes may
have converting power. But it is not the gospel. Hence, when
preaching, the minister will need to take care not to testify but to
preach. To do that he should have enough knowledge of history
and tradition to be able to read the Scriptures and use them. And
the style of working, whether preaching, caring or functioning
liturgically, needs some cohesion. There have probably been in
the Church only a few, if any, such golden days when everything
hung together. But it is undoubtedly the case that from an examined exposure of our theological thinking to pastoral ministry
(it is usually done the other way – exposing our ministry to theological scrutiny) we could improve both liturgical activities,
preaching and pastoral care itself.

CHAPTER TWO

The atonement:
for us and for our salvation

Specifically religious and common human experience coincide in the moral, social and spiritual dilemmas that confront human beings. St Paul, for example, agonizes that, in spite of the advantages of birth, status, faith and teaching, he finds himself willing one course of action and pursuing another (Romans 7). He does not speak for the religious person alone; here he is everyone. Job, sitting in the ashes of his life, surrounded by friends who grind him further into the dust, is not just the archetypal man of faith. He is everyone who has known the bitterness of undeserved suffering and its unremitting pressure, which can reduce all comment to banality.

AMBIVALENCE AND AMBIGUITY

Human life is intrinsically insecure and uncertain. We live, therefore, with our ambivalence and in the midst of ambiguity. Indeed, these are two quintessential themes of modern life. Found primarily in literary criticism and psychology, they describe a new awareness in human beings. 'Ambiguity' refers to the way that each situation is suffused with options that are not obviously distinguishable in value. 'Ambivalence' speaks of the opposed attitudes, feelings or values which the individual may find in tension within himself, tearing him apart. For many these are also prominent factors in religious belief; it is simultaneously important and unimportant, true but untrue, vital but unnecessary, restorative and destructive. In our ambiguous context we find ourselves ambivalent, as we grapple with the meaning of Christian commitment and behaviour.

HOW WE ACHIEVE ANYTHING

'Ambiguity' and 'ambivalence' sound undesirable. They conjure up a picture of people who dither when decisiveness is needed. Yet the way that we handle them is the foundation of action both by individuals and by organizations. One of our earliest developmental experiences is to discover that we cannot fall back upon mother for ever. It is part of growing up that we learn to leave her in order to make adult relationships. We do not want to go but have to act and to grow through this struggle with her. We also learn that we cannot always resolve crises through reflection on ourselves and putting our internal self into order. The outside world impinges with such force that we have to respond to it and its impact on our inner world. We may, therefore, have to act, even though it may seem irrationally, but at least to some effect.

The key to this side of our behaviour lies in the way that we relate to the external world. Our actions there are marked by projective behaviour. This appears in the everyday experience of locating in others faults (or more rarely virtues) which we cannot acknowledge in ourselves. But although this may be a technique for defending ourselves against something which we dislike or feel to be threatening, the outcome is that we are confronted with choice. We may acknowledge that part of ourself which we are projecting on to the other and try to do something about it. Or we may split ourselves from it, leave it in the other person and try to avoid it and the associated anxieties.

Whenever we face choice, we confront our own ambivalence. This feeling also originates in our first experience of the world as composed of good and bad objects. We respond by a split within ourselves, love or hate. At first it is beyond our capacity to hold these objects and emotions at the same time. In normal development, however, we learn to do this and to cope with the range of associated feelings. 'Ambivalence' refers to this ability to hold love and hate, good and bad together. But this is not a simple progression. We do not entirely abandon one phase as we move to the next; the primitive parts of ourselves survive, and somewhere, underlying our ordinary ambivalence, the violence of the earlier stage still rages.

We also see this ambivalence in groups, where it appears as fight/flight behaviour. This is fight *and* flight; it is not simply one or other. Aggressive fight or fearful flight are always simultaneous possibilities. The words that describe this clearly come from a military background. Certainly in battle a regiment can switch with surprising speed from one to the other. We acknowledge this in the phrase 'turning point'. A change occurs over a long period. But there comes a moment when we feel (and often only understand on reflection) that an especially significant event occurred.

Example: the Battle of Britain

This battle in the Second World War lasted from 10 July until 17 September 1940. Throughout that period there were daily engagements between the Luftwaffe and the Royal Air Force. But on 15 August a major encounter left the Germans severely damaged. It was the turning point, though no one knew it and the fighting continued. But the air battle that day was the point at which things changed, as it were, in a moment.

The fact that this single underlying assumption itself contains the two possibilities of fight and flight reminds us how complex this world is. We have to mobilize these ambivalent parts of ourselves, whether individually or in a group, in order to achieve anything. But implicitly at the same time, because of this ambivalence, we are emotionally uncertain about what to do. Projective behaviour, for example, may have two outcomes – either attachment to or rejection of what we project. These are parallel to the dynamic of fight/flight in a group. When one is active, the other may be obscured, but only temporarily.

Example: the new convert

Recent converts often illustrate this phenomenon. They rapidly become eager evangelists as, highly motivated by new-found faith, they seek to convert all around them to their own experience. They cannot conceive that others might not share the experience that they have. But they are also the most vulnerable to the collapse of that belief when they come up against anything unexpected or unfamiliar. This decline is described in several ways – lack of depth, shortage of experience, or needing time to consolidate belief.

But another way of seeing it is in terms of unconscious projective behaviour, by which unresolved tensions and anxieties in the convert's religious experience (which is itself at an early stage) are projected on to others and dealt with there, usually with enthusiastic aggression. Converts' behaviour is ambiguous because they have not yet come to terms with the ambivalences that lie at the root of all religious experience, including theirs. When this phenomenon appears in a congregation or committee, the double dynamic of fight/flight prevails. A heightened sense of excitement and anxiety is coupled with inevitable uncertainty. The behaviour of such a group, even when the underlying dynamic is discerned, is uncannily unpredictable.

AMBIGUITY AND THE CROSS

There can be little doubt to which article of Christian faith this dynamic relates: it is the cross, the symbol of Christianity and the atonement. Nothing in the Christian faith seems more secure. It is a focus for commitment, creating demand and support for the believer and impressing itself upon the non-believer. Yet central though this belief is, no single doctrine of that cross has ever been promulgated as orthodox. It is true that some small churches and sects have made the meaning of atonement a testing point for eligibility for memberhip. But even there the songs and hymns still ring with rich and varied metaphors.

By contrast the incarnation and the trinity have both been formulated and consolidated in creeds. But the cross and the atonement have been left free from definition. The cross is central and essential. Without it there is nothing identifiably Christian. Yet its precise meaning and significance have been left undefined. It is as if the Church at large has throughout its history successfully avoided the temptation to diminish its emotional impact.

Claims about the cross are also ambiguous. It is described in the same breath as victory and defeat, achievement and failure, the end of one man's delusion and the moment of salvation for all humankind. It is the persistent problem and the persistent symbol. This may explain why, as seems to happen at critical junctures in the Church's history, the generally accepted understanding of the atonement becomes unsatisfactory. We are probably at one such junction now:

> Traditional doctrines of atonement are a source of deep dissatisfaction to almost all sensitive Christians. Their transactional character, whether expressed in terms of propitiation, substitution, or payment of a debt, make them an easy target for criticism. Yet the cross of Christ remains a powerful source of the experience of forgiveness and renewal.[1]

This power is apparent in the two approaches to the atonement which for a thousand years, or so, have dominated Western thought. For the first thousand years Christians scarcely attempted a coherent doctrine. The prevailing image – an analogy or parable, rather than a theory – was of *Christus victor*, the triumphant Christ who paid a ransom, often, but not always, to the devil for mankind's salvation. The moral problem represented by the powerful experience of oppressive evil was firmly left with God.

Example: Laudes regiae

This fine piece of elaborated plainsong was probably sung at coronations in Winchester and elsewhere on festivals. The refrain is:

Christus vincit, Christus regnat, Christus imperat (Christ conquers, Christ reigns, Christ rules)

There follow prayers and acclamations:

King of kings, our king, our glory, our help, our strength; Our freedom and redemption, our invincible victory.

The theme is 'victory', and it sums up the theological ambience within which *Christus victor* sustained the Church.

Subsequently, however, two main streams of interpretation can be discerned.

Anselm

The first is based on Anselm's theory of satisfaction. He was Archbishop of Canterbury when, during a political struggle, he was forced to leave. It was during this suffering that he wrote his influential book *Cur Deus homo?* (Why did God become human?) It is juridical, about fairness and penalty. Its weaknesses have often been identified: it reverses the biblical stance that the cross reconciled man to God, and presents a view of God as the one who needs reconciling; man becomes isolated from creation as a whole; salvation is achieved by his escaping an awesome God to find refuge in a loving Christ. From this theological ground, the theory of penal substitution emerges. According to this view, God, having no choice but to punish sin, accepts the sacrifice of Christ in place of the death of men and women. It is a doctrine which is chiefly associated with evangelicalism. It has its own internal logic but does not work well as a metaphor, since it requires that justice becomes apparently injustice.

Yet this view of the cross and atonement has enabled men and women to believe that their personal freedom and survival are guaranteed, however oppressive the forces ranged against them, and to act accordingly. The cost is felt to be borne by God in Jesus Christ, even though logically the real cost may turn out to be to God's credibility. Yet the individual's sense of being saved can be so intense that the further consequences of this theory are left unexamined. There is, therefore, something about the ambiguity of God, as he is presented in this penal theory, which serves the believer. Because the penal theory preserves the two central aspects of the cross, ambiguity and cost, it has outlasted (and still survives) the attacks made on its reasonableness or its biblical credentials.

Abelard

Anselm lived c.1033–1109. Almost his contemporary was Peter Abelard, 1079–1142. Professor of theology in Paris, he too worked on the atonement, and the 'subjectivist' approach is attributed to him. Beholding the cross, men and women may see the love of God poured out in Christ's death, absorb that love, and become conformed to it. The love of God displayed in the dying Christ evokes an answering love in the person who contemplates it. It is a view which has consistent power, but which is vulnerable as a theory to the general criticism that the component of justice, which is implicit in the biblical traditions about the cross, is too severely diminished. But the issue of cost re-emerges. The believer experiences salvation as a change of heart, but the cost of bringing about that change seems out of all proportion to the effect. It is too easy to think of alternative ways, and the need for the crucifixion does not remain apparent. Yet this view, too, has been and still is effective in generating saving love, because, although very different from Anselm's theory, it too preserves the twin essentials of the cross – ambiguity and cost.

Today

Contemporary thinking about the cross seems to be moving back behind such theorizing. The theme of sacrifice has re-emerged. Although the practice is remote from the modern world, the concept is widely used. One way in which the concept of sacrifice is employed today is in the concept of 'scapegoat'. For example, in family therapy this word describes the member of the family who is sacrificed by the others in order to save themselves having to face aspects of their individual and social behaviour. The idea of sacrifice has often lain dormant beneath the surface of social consciousness. But from time to time it re-emerges to illuminate a facet of common human experience which is in danger of being overlooked or denied.

The themes of autonomy and alienation and the sense of being abandoned by God (and abandoning him) also permeate recent reflection on humankind and the innocently dying Christ. The cross becomes the place of God's death, both in the sense of the death of the old gods of theism and the place where Jesus, and hence all mankind, experiences the death (or absence) of God. The cry of dereliction resonates with much in modern art, music and literature. The suffering God, who shares in some fashion the agonies of his creation, seems to have become, in spite of difficulties, a theological necessity. God not only fully experiences the ultimate human limitation – death – but also the spiritual finitude of God-abandonedness. The outcome is neither despair nor adulation. But the consequences are found in today's theological and human crises. In the death of God we again observe ambiguity linked with a sense of cost being publicly borne.

SCRUTINIZED BY THE CROSS

Throughout the history of the atonement one point regularly emerges: whenever it becomes the focus for reflection, imagination or theorizing, the crude fact of the cross itself becomes critically active. Every meditation and theological elaboration upon the cross becomes itself scrutinized by the cross. Every theory or theology undergoes a reflexive test from the cross. And with Luther we dare even suggest that God himself is examined by the cross: 'The cross puts everything to the test. Blessed is he who understands.'[2] No theory is sufficient which does not offer an idea about how salvation is achieved and at what cost. The achievement, and some criteria of what that is, have to be incorporated in any understanding. Moreover, the ambiguous nature of the cross is effective for others only in so far as it questions itself. And it is intrinsic to the cross that, while explanation must be attempted, it remains inexplicable and unexplained. When any theological interpretation seems to diminish that ambiguity, even if for a time it seems clear and powerful, it too eventually comes under judgement. Those, therefore, who are to be saved through the cross of Christ must be allowed to be conscious of their own ambivalent feelings and attitudes towards this symbol.

We can clarify this general observation into four major issues which arise from reflection upon this Christian essential.

Necessary inadequacy

Every theory of the cross and the atonement must have inadequacy built into it. This may arise from a particular cultural conditioning. The ransom view, for example, relies upon a specific stance towards Scripture; Anselm's interpretation depends to a large extent upon the social structures of his age; Peter Abelard reacts against the prevailing theologies that he was required to teach, yet needed to experience a loving relationship with Heloise before he could articulate his own understanding; Frances Young, a contemporary professor of theology and the mother of a handicapped child, intertwines the two and convincingly demonstrates the renewed cultural context for sacrifice. Jürgen Moltmann, another theologian, was a young German prisoner of war when the Second World War ended, and has had to respond to the contemporary crisis of identity and relevance which he discerns in the light of his experience.

It is beyond question that views of the cross are culturally conditioned; but it is noticeable that they are not culturally confined. The drawing power of penal theories persists in spite of social changes. Abelard's stance still attracts because of the perennial beauty of human intimacy and love. Even sacrifice, which has little obvious connection with today's world – for example in work with families – can come alive. Of all major Christian themes the cross is the most culturally conditioned and historically located. The crucifixion is set in history in a way that incarnation, creation and resurrection are not. The once-for-all character of the atonement is notable. Yet this cross is the distinctive Christian symbol and forms the continuing point of judgement on all in every age who claim status as Christian.

Undefined and undefinable

Second, the Church has not sought to define an official doctrine of the atonement. This is not only an effect of the cross on Christian practice and theology, but also demonstrates the evangelical mode of the gospel of the cross. St Paul claimed that 'we preach Christ and him crucified' (1 Corinthians 1.23); alternatively the cross may be presented as the means of religious, cultural or political revolution. But in each way the cross is the distinctive demand of the gospel. Because it addresses the world at large, and the Christian community specifically, the cross cannot endure being overlaid with theory, and the Church's instinct to resist endorsing one dogma witnesses to this critical function.

Achievement

Third, the cross is always associated with a specific achievement. It may be that the world is changed, the radical disjunction of sin is overcome, or sacrifice is effectively ordered. But all emphasize achievement through the cross. The phrase 'the work of Christ' usually refers to his passion and death, even though a sounder theological stance would perhaps apply it to the whole range of his incarnation, life, death and resurrection. There is also the obvious, but often overlooked fact that all four Gospels give a disproportionate space to the last week or so of Jesus' life. But even in that larger context the cross and passion are the fulcrum on which the arguments turn, or the lens through which the other aspects of Christ are given clear reference and meaning.

Suffering

Finally, there are pain and suffering. No interpretation which lessens or removes the reality of Christ's agony and death has survived for long. The reality of that suffering has repeatedly been reaffirmed in three ways. First, we note that Jesus experienced physical pain like any other victim of a crucifixion. The Gospels do not minimize this, and the imagery has proved rich for art and devotion. At times of disenchantment with theology this aesthetic view has sustained the cross at the centre of Christian belief, life and devotion. Today we also know from archaeological finds how a crucified man physically died slowly drowning with fluid in his lungs.

Second, we perceive the suffering associated with sin. All theories of the atonement are concerned with sin and forgiveness. The need to make amends for faults or the wish for cleansing in the face of divine purity are taken into the death of Christ. The arguments are about the means; the end is not disputed. When a highly personalized sense of sin is explored, the intense experience of guilt is also related closely to the cross. This accounts for the continuing attraction of the satisfaction and substitutionary theories. Although the precise means by which the death of Christ deals with man's guilt may remain unclear, the experience of liberation or salvation is such that inconsistencies in the doctrine are tolerated.

Third, we recognize that pain and suffering involve cost. Here the isolation of the cross from its theological context can prove dangerous. Devotion to the passion and to images of purely human suffering can become morbidly narcissistic. Yet a strong sense of cost is crucial to any awareness of the cross, theoretical, emotional or aesthetic, and nowhere is this more evoked than in meditation on the pain and suffering inflicted.

These four issues in the doctrine of the atonement indicate the essential ambiguity of the cross. There is a tension in two directions, which, if resolved in favour of either, the fact of the cross itself immediately reintroduces: it is the core of the Church's proclamation, but it is also the stumbling-block of the gospel.

THE FELT ATONEMENT

The term 'mystery' may be too easily used in connection with the cross. But it points us in the right direction, since mysteries are felt, not understood. The cross and atonement, too, cannot be considered apart from the various feelings of those involved, both then in the story and now through belief. The Gospel narratives put physical and psychological feelings at the core of their accounts. In the passion narratives the people who surround Jesus become rounded characters. Up to that point we have been given evidence for the kingdom of God, which is disclosed through nameless lepers, an anonymous young ruler or an unknown Syrophoenician woman – interesting people whose faith and responses to Jesus contribute to our identifying who he is and maybe even in some way to his own self-discovery and therefore ours. We inevitably speculate about them, but we have little information or detail.

By contrast, however, as the passion story begins, the characters become named, vulnerable and feeling people: Pilate and his wife; Caiaphas and the priests and their human jealousies; Joseph of Arimathea and his secret faith; Peter, the head disciple, who flees, and Judas, who comes, drawing close, to hand over his Lord. Even an unimportant servant, Malchus, is eventually given a name and role in the tradition. It is as if we now must have fully human beings standing in their own right. The sense of mystery which we associate with the cross arises from an instinctive sense that, as these people, with their passions, uncertainties, desires and feelings, become so much more evidently human beings, then, when we think of God's own involvement in this event, we may be nudging what may riskily be termed 'the feeling side of God'.

This point has been reaffirmed in contemporary theologies of the crucified God. Moltmann, for example, following Luther, points out that the primary function of Christ's cross is discernment of reality. Since 'the test of everything is the cross', the 'everything' includes the question 'What does the cross of Jesus mean for God himself?' as part of the question of what the cross means for humankind, in particular for me.

A similar vein runs through reflection of a less theologically sophisticated kind. It is, therefore, wise to trust instinct, and enquire about the implications of such thinking. For instance, the apparent conflict between the so-called subjective (Abelard) and objective (Anselm) theories of the atonement diminishes. Feelings expressed in devotion to the crucified one have instinctively refused to admit a distinction. Two familiar and traditional forms of prayer – meditation and contemplation – normally complement each other.[3] And this is especially true of meditation on the crucified one and the self-awareness that follows through contemplation. The reason for this may lie in the way in which the atonement raises the level of our consciousness of and questioning about the feeling side of God as this is displayed in the crucified Christ. Matching feelings are generated in ourselves, and the distinction between his 'objective' work and our 'subjective' response ceases to feel significant.

These double or ambivalent feelings, with which God involves himself in the atonement, are powerful and frequently confusing. But they also represent the part of ourselves which we have to harness for any achievement. They are powerful because they originate within the earliest phase in our development as human beings, the psychological bedrock of who we are. But without these primitive emotions and the managing of chaotic experience into some sort of order – the acknowledgement of ambivalence – we should not possess the facets of a human existence which produce results. These include all the risky aspects of life – creating an attitude of healthy suspicion and questioning, forming ideals, and sustaining the effort to act.

To achieve anything, we have to deal with the world outside us, which we might regard as 'objective'. But as we do so, we become increasingly aware that it is not all 'out there'. We are handling our internal worlds, or what we might label the 'subjective' aspect to life at the same time. We therefore become anxious about both our inner selves and the outside world. Interaction between them is necessary for any achievement, but it is also implicitly dangerous. But the more aware we become of that, the more our anxiety increases. Sometimes it becomes too much, and we revert to the comforting debilitation of immature dependence.

Example: Gethsemane

The Gospel story of Jesus' agony in the Garden of Gethsemane provides a fine illustration of this interaction. The choices before Jesus lie between fight (which the disciple with the sword acts out on behalf of everyone) and flight (in which finally all the disciples indulge). Their behaviour is that of a group locked into feelings alone, what we might today call 'basic assumption-based' behaviour. It is unable to harness them to some useful purpose. As a result the disciples collapse into childlike dependence upon Jesus at the very moment when he is least likely to be able to respond effectively. Anxiously they look to him to resolve the problems and doubts which increasingly press on them just when he is most occupied with his own self and his response to external circumstances. As a result, all the actions in the Garden, instead of achieving something positive, act like lightning conductors to remove power from all. The disciples' dependence is focused upon Jesus, and when he fails to meet their expectations of powerful leadership through divine intervention, they are lost. He is left alone to explore what that fight and flight and the feelings of ambivalence and ambiguity mean – ultimately crucifixion.

The account also suggests, however, that Jesus has prepared himself for this in his earlier praying. Struggling with God he realizes that, if he himself shifts into that dependent mode of behaviour and surrenders his responsibility for his actions to God, nothing will be achieved. So we are told of ambivalence in his praying. He is caught between on the one hand the immature dependence of unconsidered surrender to God and on the other hand taking a responsible decision to do what must be done, harnessing his dependence in a mature fashion to the task in hand. A deepening awareness dawns that this means that there will be casualties, chief among which may be his intimacy with God. But at the same time this may be the cost of any achievement.

This is precisely what Christians find in their reflection on the cross. Both in the theological tradition and in our own experience it resists every attempt at understanding, whether religious, cultic, mystical or ethical, because each diminishes its stark horror. They divert attention from feelings to believed understanding, as people demand that God be the God they wish him to be: one who escapes crucifixion. In the story of Gethsemane the disciples act out this resolution of basic anxiety while Jesus supports the ambivalence. Similarly in the history of Christian spirituality there has been pressure to soften the reality of the cross by inviting God to accede to our dependent wish not to be involved. But through the persistent theme that there is no ultimate interpretation of the cross, God protects the necessary ambivalence of fight/flight against the pressures towards persistent dependence. Therefore, there remains hope of action, whatever the change may be that we call salvation.

THE TRANSACTION OF THE CROSS: EVIL AND GUILT

The massive problems of evil and guilt focus in the cross. The idea of a devil has been used on occasions to keep evil apart from God, and this is the core of *Christus victor*, Christ the conqueror. Alternatively, evil may be reduced to personal sin and in the mystery of the cross handled through private meditation, confession and absolution. But neither type of approach feels tolerable in the face of the scale of actual evil which our generations continue to experience and which earlier ages called cosmic.

The Jewish experience

The question is so large that any attempt to explain seems to trivialize it. Casual Christian discussion of intolerable evil and suffering in the light of the cross tends to be vapid; it also finds itself under the judgement of that cross. One means, however, by which today's Christian pastor can begin to approach this massive dimension to human life, without losing touch with the reality of evil or the theological and spiritual significance of the cross of Christ, is by reflecting on recent Jewish experience. This exercise is not novel; the first Christians did something similar when they appropriated Jewish books to form the Old Testament. Today's equivalent is to take recent Jewish experience in the twentieth century as data.

By 'experience' Jewish writers mean something like 'interpreted feeling'. Contemplating the Nazi attempt to exterminate the Jews in Europe, a conclusion has to be reached. It is not enough merely to record the raw data, which we might call 'the experience'. Interpretation of some sort is needed so that profound emotions can be integrated with reflection and so become distinctively 'Jewish'. This leads to a series of competing standpoints – the dying Jews were atoning on behalf of mankind's sins; the camps were the place of God's revelation, where he reaffirmed his faithfulness to the covenant; God ceased to exist after Auschwitz; or the whole episode is another instance of the unknowable plan of an inscrutable God. They raise the questions about God, the scale of evil, and the atonement which contemporary Christianity must address, although no Christian may presume to judge between these approaches. The choice lies starkly between the cross (or the Holocaust, which itself means 'whole burning', that is, a great sacrifice) as the place where a window opens upon God or where he finally denies himself.

A window into God

A window forms part of a wall, letting the light in and allowing people to look 'through the wall'. When a window is incorporated, a wall ceases to be a barrier between us and the outside world; it becomes a boundary across which transactions can be effected. Through it we look out at the world outside. We do not enter that world, but bring it through the clear glass across the boundary of the wall into our inside world.

When considering God and the problem of evil, we can regard the cross as such a window. Through it God's internal world draws into itself what seems separate from or outside him – that is, evil at its most excruciatingly powerful and inscrutable. At the same time the cross also opens up the inside world of God to those who are caught up in and dominated by so much evil. He invites us to see him making this awesome 'other' world of evil his own. This is where the traditional idea of transaction, which is associated with atonement, fits.

THE AESTHETIC TRANSACTION AND FANTASY

Transaction between God and evil (however that is defined) lies deep in the doctrine of the atonement. It has proved, however, to be a focal point around which fantasy has most easily developed. In this field, where imagination reigns, powerful images in art, drama and music have been produced. They have stimulated and sustained belief and guided the way that people think and live. But with the psychoanalytic developments of the twentieth century the world of fantasy has been examined and exposed, and we are less confident in it than were our predecessors. However, this is no reason for abandoning the significance of fantasy. We need to consider the modern contributions to its understanding and see what they may add to our theological reflection.

Fantasy is not a whim or an eccentricity. It may contain elements of wish-fulfilment, but it is more than that. At one time 'fantasy' was frequently contrasted with 'reality' and its value diminished accordingly. Now, however, we begin again to realize that the world of fantasy and the 'real' world are not opposed. We construct our world through the interplay of both, just as we live in the interaction of conscious and unconscious minds. Fantasy, therefore, is an important factor in our natural existence. The distorting function of evil is always at work, implied whenever evil is focused in a single being. For example, there were (and may still be) seven archangels to do God's bidding – Michael, Gabriel, Raphael, Uriel, Raguel and Sariel and another. Their number, seven of them, significantly stands for order and completeness. But the world is not like that; for one is missing – Lucifer, the great fallen one. If we are to know anything about God, his creation and our salvation, we know it will never be complete or perfect.

Unexamined fantasies, however, tend to undermine the significance of the issue that they are being generated to handle. For example, even if we operate with a less personalized notion of evil than is implied by the title 'devil', it may be so fantasized as to be assigned a matching status with God. Christian thought is prone to this sort of dualism. Not surprisingly, therefore, the devil has an uncanny knack of emerging as a more attractive, more competent and usually more powerful figure than God himself. Yet instinctively through worship and through use of Scripture and the Christian tradition we sense that this is not just a theological error. Something more profound is out of joint. While we may have moments in which we give up hope, the tradition in which we stand and the better moments in our experience assert that the world is not simply evil. Or, as we might say, a fantasy which has developed for good reason (the experience of evil) has lost touch with reality, in this case God, in whom the Christian trusts.

The issue, however, is more complex. Evil is enormous, but it resonates with the small worlds of our selves. In order to comprehend it at all, we instinctively feel we have to locate it in some being who is beyond redemption, whether a supremely evil man or a devil. But at the same time such evil cannot be easily personalized, since it seems to be on such a cosmic scale that it overwhelms our idea of what is personal, including even God himself. To think about evil at all, therefore, we need fantasy. This may explain the impressive range of imagery that accrues around the figure of a devil and why the idea of transaction has so often been focused upon him. When living with fantasy, we need to discover reality, whatever the difficulty and the cost. If atonement, the reintegration of all creation, is to come about, we must be able to recognize reality in our notion both of God and of what he deals with.

Many of the post-Auschwitz Jewish theologians have grasped this on our behalf: either their various conceptions of God have to be abandoned or the reality of evil (represented by the Holocaust) has to be perceived as a specific manifestation of God. Transaction in the atonement, therefore, is not between God and some other figure, such as the devil. It is between God, in his role as the creator of this world, and the fundamental realities of that creation, which are our experience of it – pain, suffering, evil and death. These cannot be diminished in importance or set aside. They are among the products of God's self-giving in creation. It may be that Paul in Romans 8 is feeling after this when he points out that we are not freed from decay – that is an aspect of creation – but from bondage to it.

Simplistic imagery which creates a devil to solve this tension is merely fantasy. Evil ceases to be any particular person's responsibility – mine, the devil's or God's. As such, while this stance may give momentary relief, it cannot address the awesome reality of pain and suffering in a world where we are now all victims.

GOD TRANSACTS WITH GOD

The transaction in the atonement occurs between God and himself. All transactions include certain common marks. Through this process people jointly create something new in which they invest themselves. It is marked by movement as the parties give and receive; and it is not an end itself but brings about change. Each of these characteristics is discernible in the atonement. God does not struggle with something (evil) or someone (the devil) other than himself. Nor does he invite us to join in disposing of our sin, evil and guilt by projection into that object or being. Instead, in the cross God acknowledges a profound reality of the world which he has created, accepting it as his responsibility along with the associated pain and suffering.

The basis of atonement lies in the freedom of his creatures, for the consequences of which God takes public responsibility on the cross. The Gospel stories of the crucifixion all give this freedom prominence. Peter is free to stay faithful to Jesus or deny him, and he decides; Judas is free to hand his leader over and to commit suicide; Pilate, Caiaphas, the crowd, the soldiers, and the disciples are all given permission to act autonomously. Although in each Gospel Jesus, as he moves to Jerusalem, generates a sense of destiny, there is scarcely a hint that the participants in the drama lose their freedom to be and do what they wish. They are allowed, indeed encouraged, to exercise it freely. The cumulative effect is the cross. Freedom does not belong to individuals alone. Each actor is caught up in wider networks than he or she knows, but that fact does not take away their responsibility for their own actions, some of which are mistaken and which induce feelings of guilt.

Sometimes these feelings become very confused and we slide into a pathological state which requires treatment. But a sense of guilt is not necessarily unfortunate or morbid, needing to be removed or explained away. It is the inevitable corollary of the exercise of our freedom as human beings. Such felt guilt, therefore, is a prerequisite of responsible action.

GOD'S RESPONSIBILITY AND THE CROSS

We can now begin to identify that for which God takes public responsibility in the cross. The Christian proclamation often implies that there God takes upon himself responsibility for everything and everyone. But that line of argument leads to the charge that Christianity glorifies God only at the expense of human dignity. If without consulting me God assumes responsibility for what is genuinely my concern (and for which from time to time I properly feel guilty), then the charge is just. The loss of responsibility may remove the sense of guilt, but it does so at the expense of my self-esteem and value as a being created and affirmed by God himself. Salvation then proves delusory. The other result of this implicit devaluing of what is human is a Christianity which reduces the vast dimension of human pain by comparing it with the sufferings of Christ. In my morbid moments I can then believe that in some fashion I, because of my slight anguishes, can identify with him. There is no gospel here for a world which is psychologically aware, if not always psychologically sophisticated.

In the cross God acknowledges his responsibility for the context within which our freedom to choose is made possible and for the fact that this choice is open to us. He does not deprive us of the responsibility which we feel and know to be ours or of the sense of guilt that accompanies any failure to exercise it. But by publicly proving responsibility for the fact and possibility of human freedom, he provides a reference point outside our human condition. This we can use to orientate our confused sense of guilt and thus break the inexorable cycle of despair.

THE DRAW OF THE CROSS

As if we are looking through a window, we participate in the drama of the cross, whatever the theological interpretation, by watching. The result is that it serves as a point for constructive confession. Hamlet remarked on the intimate connection between observation and drama, guilt and confession:

> I have heard
> That guilty creatures sitting at a play
> Have, by the very cunning of the scene,
> Been struck so to the soul that presently
> They have proclaimed their malefactions.
> (Hamlet 2.2.586–90)

We are invited by the drama of the cross, which inhibits too much extensive theorizing about it, to confess those feelings of guilt and inadequacy which in our reflective moments oppress us. We are also offered a specific place in the context of God's overall activity where we can locate this turmoil. Confession, therefore, is not a generalized attitude towards a generally available God. It is given specific shape and content by being located in the God of the cross of Christ.

We can now better identify the transaction in the cross. We are not invited there to surrender to God our freedom as creatures and our consequent responsibility for our failures and successes, our sin and guilt. Nor does he somehow lift that responsibility from us. If that were so, the cross could drive us only to ultimate despair, since it would deprive us of our status as creatures. This is, incidentally, why some preaching of the cross has short-term effectiveness. It panders to the immature dependent longings of the inadequate, who seek relief from realities about themselves or about the world in which they are set. Such a gospel may occasionally feel beneficial; but it will not save those who are sensitive to their autonomy and responsibility, even if they do not realize that these are gifts of the creator God. On the cross, by contrast, God accepts the consequences of our exercise of the freedom which he has assigned us – the fact and content of our freedom as creatures.

TRANSFORMED FREEDOM

From this act of atonement emerges transformed freedom. Our human bias (or sin) is to assume that our autonomy (or freedom) originates in ourselves. We treat it as a right or possession belonging to each of us. But after the cross freedom can no longer be an exercised right, with the unexpected consequences of a sense of confusion and guilt. These feelings remain, but instead of being parts of human existence to be explained or removed, they become the avenue to a new quality of life. From being destructive, or at best unfortunate, by-products of human responsibility, they become the focal point of new creative possibilities. Since human beings are freed from having to feel responsible for the fact that they are responsible, they can more confidently take authority for their lives and the consequences of their behaviour. In brief, they can afford to risk being wrong because they know that they are forgiven. New and unpredictable results ensue when such authority is exercised.

RECONCILIATION THROUGH THE CROSS

A window, however, like a transaction, works in two directions. If the cross exposes to us the origins of our freedom in God, it also allows us to perceive how God takes into his inner life the cost of this gift. Any effective action involves cost, and the doctrine of the atonement is above all about achievement or salvation. The cross suggests that the cost of this is nothing less than that of God's being pulled apart.

Can we speak in any sense of God being torn apart in the cross? And if we can, is it legitimate? The second question, at least, is answered by two of the Gospel writers. Matthew and Mark both hint that it is, in the cry of desolation, 'My God, my God, why have you forsaken me?' (Mark 15.34; Matthew 27.46, all versions). Luke and John, who omit this anguished question, describe Jesus' life as ending with a gasp or a cry. But these are only indicators and suggestions. If we are to take our question about God seriously, taking licence from the Gospels themselves, we must consider what such splitting might represent.

We have already noted that one means by which we deal with what is unfamiliar, and so disturbing or difficult to handle, is by separating ourselves from it. This seems to occur in two stages which for the most part are not usually distinguished. We first split and then use the mechanism of projection. For example, we identify others as 'them' over against 'us'. Black and white, worker and boss, men and women – these are obvious instances. We can hear this splitting, even in the most apparently conciliatory language, when a group of people is referred to as 'they' or 'them'. Under our many sophistications we still tend to revert to an idea of a world which is divided simplistically into good (those whom we trust will help us) and evil (those who will do us harm) in order to cope with its impossible absurdities.

Example: the barbarians

The Greek poet George Kavafis writes about a town where everyone is expecting the barbarians to come and take over. Someone, probably a child, asks why some things are happening – the emperor is in his best clothes, the senators are not passing laws, the orators are not speaking; the answer to all is that everyone is waiting for the barbarians. Towards the end of the day some people come from outside and say that there are no barbarians in sight and they won't be coming today. Indeed there may be no babarians at all. The poem ends:

Now what's going to happen to us without barbarians?
Those people were a kind of solution.[4]

If God engages with human beings, as we have reflected, he must also encounter them at the unconscious level. One characteristic of such a meeting is splitting. This behaviour, whether in an individual or a group, is not a form of debilitating weakness. It is a basic characteristic of human beings, a defence which we deploy usually in the face of imminent and overwhelming stress or destructive anxiety. It is the way we are made. That being so, we may consider what it means for God to take responsibility for the world that he has created.

The problem of evil is complex, but whatever we make of it, it is within the Christian scheme other than God. Even if it is not personalized into a devil, it stands for that which is 'not God'. There is some sort of division. The cross in this light demonstrates two points. First, it endorses this splitting as a fundamental characteristic of God's created world. No one is immune from it, and God himself affirms this givenness of what he has made by facing the pain of being pulled between what is God ('me') and what is evil ('not-me'). The process remains but is transformed. Instead of its being a defensive projection, on the cross God transforms such splitting into another means of creation and salvation.

Second, since human responsibility and its free exercise are God's gracious self-giving for us, we can never claim that they belong to us. They are assigned, not owned. It is this point that is made in Genesis when God makes humankind in his own image. That image is not something visible: that will become an idol. The image of God is of one who is free to exercise his will and also chooses how he interprets living responsibly. When God acts with such grace, one consequence is that humankind has a similar freedom. The difference is that when we act on that freedom, the consequences are sin (failure or falling short) and evil (damage to others and to our selves). So when in the cross we observe God publicly taking his responsibility for the fact and content of our freedom, he also suffers the destructiveness of evil and sin.

When the projective behaviour that results from this splitting is pointed out to us in everyday life, we feel guilty for having failed ourselves to perceive what we were doing. We wonder why

we did it in the first place and how best to act in the light of our
new perception. This anxiety may restart the defensive process,
leading to yet another split between what we will acknowledge as
ours and what we project into some other. At this level of fundamental psychological functioning there is an inevitability which
can lead to a sense of hopelessness. A cycle seems to be set up,
from which escape is impossible. We may seek solace or salvation
in greater knowledge, but this rarely seems to be effective. After
Freud, 'Never before had so many seen man's shortcomings so
clearly and been able to do so little about it.' For ourselves, let
alone for our neighbour, understanding does not necessarily lead
to forgiveness any more than learning leads to salvation.

GOD'S 'EXPERIENCE' AND OURS

Here, however, our human experience illuminates the doctrine of
the atonement. What is for us a defensive stance is given status
as a creative consequence of the freedom which God gives us. We
tend to deal with destructive sin and matching guilt, by splitting
them from ourselves and projecting them into others. By contrast, however, in the cross God holds such splitting within
himself and demonstrates how it becomes a means of redemption. The damaging effects are faced, not denied, and thus they
are transformed. It is not that they do not occur for God or that
they cease to matter. If this were the case, evil and sin would not
hold the awesome reality for us that they do. Their power lies in
their seeming to be inevitably associated with the creative sides
of ourselves, our freedom and autonomy. We are again with Paul
in Romans 7.

Reflecting on this wrenching apart, our approach to the
problem of evil is also transformed. The human tendency is to
separate evil from good, using criteria derived from whatever
belief system we adopt. It is almost intolerable to think of evil as
anything other than the opposite of good. The cross, as the focus
for all that is both good and evil, does not countenance this. It is
both God's act on behalf of his creation (which is good) and at the
same moment the destruction of God's righteous one (which is
evil). Thus evil is affirmed for what it is. There is no magical conversion of evil into good, but in all its horror and starkness it is
incorporated into God's action.

Example: Judas, a man with a mission

The enigma of Judas is a prime illustration of this process. Those who compiled the Gospels seem to have been sensitive to this theological dimension to the saga. Judas is not prominent as a bad object, although he could easily have been so presented, as later Christian traditions show. Abuse of him in the Gospels is minimal. On the other hand, the evil, that is the massive destructiveness for himself and others, in his actions is not underrated. Interestingly it is Judas's essentially human quality, neither absolutely evil nor determinedly responsible, but rather confused, misled and ultimately tragically mistaken, that ensures his place in the Gospel narratives. The whole drama of salvation from the human perspective is encapsulated in him. That is why subsequent Christians have found themselves ambivalent about him. He is so easy an object onto which to project our own guilt, especially in relation to God, and then to dismiss it. Yet at the same time, without Judas and his actions, we are without hope of salvation, since he is quintessentially in his dilemma and actions every human being, not least today. Each of us, therefore, must in the end answer the question: Can Judas be saved?

Judas's story is about evil. There is, however, also a link between this and guilt. And underlying the issue of guilt is the central problem of authority and its exercise. To take authority is a complex act. It involves both accepting the person that I am and working in the roles, many as they are, that I hold. As a concept, therefore, authority defines all that we call human: who we are; what we are; and what we are for. When we exercise authority we feel a struggle within ourselves and may come into conflict with others. The two usually go hand in hand. Concealed, therefore, in the suffering, pain, sin and guilt which are taken up in the Christian doctrine of the cross and atonement, there remains the basic human fault – divinely assigned and humanly accepted authority and the perpetual problems of its exercise.

Judas's story illuminates the problem of evil for each of us. The actions of the other disciples illustrate the link between guilt and authority. Each and all of them fail to sustain the role of disciple which Jesus had assigned them and which they had accepted. They fled. Judas takes the final way out – suicide. Peter resorts to lying when his discipleship is challenged by a maid in the courtyard. On this foundation the Church is to be built. For the group (without Judas) reassembles and discovers reconciliation and forgiveness.

THE CROSS AND FORGIVENESS

The disciples are the precursors of all who wrestle with the guilt and splitting that result from our failure to live competently with the authority which is ours as human beings. Here lies the basis of forgiveness which has always been found in the cross. It is offered in the doctrine of the atonement, through which we discover that forgiveness comes about in an unexpected way. Our natural inclination is to think of it as divine forgetfulness, to let the past go and, as we say, to forgive and forget. But the atonement demonstrates that forgiveness is explicitly found in remembering.

Honest remembrance is a specific instance of exercising our authority. It requires us to acknowledge our past and what has contributed to our being who we are. But we also have to recollect and examine our behaviour in role, and so confess as much guilt as we can recognize. This on its own might become morbid. But because of the forgiveness available through the atonement, our honest remembrance ceases to be a reason for despair, and new hopes emerge. That is another way of talking of forgiveness. It comes about because it is rooted in realities about ourselves as human beings and in the reality of God himself. The primitive urge to split in order to save ourselves is ineradicable. But when this facet of his human creation is taken by God into himself, as we see at the cross, then it is transformed from a defence to an acknowledged reality to be used for constructive living.

The cross pulls together many strands of our common human experience. But it is not just a generalized symbol of the fraught nature of human life; it is the identifiable place where God publicly aligns himself with his creature. The pain, which is so central a theme of the cross, is not undeserved pain which derives from sin or guilt which do not belong to him. Nor is it just a comforting expression of solidarity with the pain of suffering and oppressed humanity. Both ideas are rich and powerfully suggestive, stimulating spiritual development and inspired action. Ultimately, however, they do not impinge upon common human experience at a sufficiently profound level for the cross to be God's saving activity for all his creatures. For, as any pastor knows, many people do not feel oppressed and not all live with a profound sense of sin and guilt. If the pain of the cross is to be a factor in the salvation of all men and women, it cannot be linked to only one fragment of the experience of some. Now, however, we see that in the cross God aligns himself with the fundamental experience of life which is common to us all – the evil and guilt inevitably linked with our exercise of our authority as human beings, which itself derives from our being creatures within God's creation.

SUBSTITUTION AND REPRESENTATION

One further theme in this doctrine remains to be noted – the representative nature of the death of Christ. 'Substitution' still causes lively controversy and must be considered in any account of the atonement.

> In social life, substitution is a universal phenomenon, both in conduct and in its outcome. If substitution is not a universal phenomenon in human social relationships, if the individualistic interpretation of responsibility and recompense need not be rejected as one-sided because it overlooks the social relationships of individual behaviour, then it is not possible to speak meaningfully of a vicarious character to the fate of Jesus Christ.[5]

Even if Christ's death is unique and distinctive, it must nevertheless have a vicarious effect. Otherwise it remains yet one more example of a tragic and unjustified death, albeit one which has shaped much of Western culture. To invite people to observe, meditate upon and use in the ordering of their lives the horror of one specific crucifixion appears selfish and hollow. Representation, therefore, is an essential theme to be retained at the heart of the doctrine of the atonement.

Today, however, in this respect, as in many others, we lack a conceptual framework with which to make sense of vicarious suffering and death. The process of rejecting any such notion began at the Enlightenment and, although some Christians still resist it, it has reached fruition in our present age. Humankind's horrendous record, compounded by widespread knowledge of it through the media, has had a profound impact equally on Christian theological study and pastoral sensitivity. We can, however, sustain a genuine sense of substitution if we conceive representation as a function within a relationship. In relationships people do not substitute for each other in the sense of replacement. But they do act on behalf of one another and so represent, or appropriately substitute for, one another.

Example: the family

A marriage or a family works well so long as the participants are willing to be allowed to act on behalf of each other. No single member does everything. But, what is more difficult, they need also to be prepared to delegate responsibility to one another and, when necessary, to others beyond their immediate circle. For instance, parents have to allow others to represent aspects of themselves to their children – teachers, to whom they delegate important learning; doctors, who are given responsibility for health; or baby-sitters, entrusted with the child's security. Indeed a grasp of this is a sign of maturity both in the individuals concerned and in the growth of the family unit itself. For it shows that we are sufficiently confident in ourselves and others to be able to entrust aspects of ourselves to them.

But the next step in delegation is more delicate and consequently more hazardous and difficult to accept. We also have to become sufficiently assured to be able to allow others to take aspects of ourselves without our permission. This is far from controlled or managed delegation; it is surrender of control. This comes about when we can recognize that we may unwittingly be asked to do things on behalf of another (or, as it is more pejoratively described, that we may be used) and remain content with being so used. We accept that we are objects for other people's projections, and that people are acting on them; that roles, which have not been negotiated, are being attributed to us; and, put brutally, that we are more than likely being manipulated. This is not a comfortable form of substitution, but it is an integral part of social and personal life.

Thus the substitutionary aspect of Christ's death is not that he takes mankind's place in general or mine in particular. For many people, perhaps most, such an idea is at best difficult and, even worse, immoral. It deprives us of that responsibility which we discover in many contexts is central to our human existence. So, far from bringing life, this sort of proposed atonement actually brings death.

In Greek the little words count. Two prepostions are *anti* and *hyper*: the first means 'in place of' and the second means 'on behalf of'. The second is most frequently used of God's activity, including the cross.[6] Christ does not die instead of me; he dies on my behalf. There is a difference. If he just replaces me, then I become no participant in the event of the cross. If, by contrast, we understand that he does so on my behalf, I am not excluded. The point is made by the conversion experience of Baron von Hügel. One day he found himself standing in front of the picture of the crucified Christ, who said: 'All this I have done for you; what have you done for me?' He was profoundly moved and changed, for he saw Christ acting on his behalf, neither excusing him nor accusing him, but inviting him to join him by taking up his own cross. God's cross stands consistently for divine willingness to be used and to accept the corollaries of misuse and abuse.

This is one outcome of the abandonment of the defence of splitting and its transformation into a creative stance. Assigned roles, over which there is no chance to negotiate, are accepted. This does not, however, imply mere passivity. That can give, and has at times given, rise to a pathetic Christianity marked more by masochism than mission. Accepting roles generated by the projections of others still allows opportunity for their being identified, responded to and so interpreted. In the case of the cross, that interpretation is not just in terms of the attempts at doctrinal understanding which have gone on since the earliest days. It is also a function of that starkness of the cross itself, whatever image of it we create, which we noted at the opening of this chapter.

When we see substitution in terms of such willingness to be used, however unjust and improper the use, we are offered an effective way by which there is hope of reconciliation, or constructive interrelating, between people and between mankind and God. This is what the cross and atonement affirm: to follow the way of the cross is to accept responsibility for the evil and guilt which results from my life as myself and in my roles and, even more, for the fact that I am usable by others, whether wittingly or unwittingly, and to endure the consequent cost. Here the bridge between the cross and the continuing ministry of atonement is found. For use, abuse and misuse are definitions of a ministry which embodies and thus makes present the way of the cross.

CONCLUSION

The felt experiences of human life coincide in the ultimately indefinable doctrine of the atonement: it is unfair, unjust and rationally indefensible. Nevertheless, we persist with the cross and atonement, not for any benefit to the self, but on behalf of, or for the benefit of, others; and the cost is borne, usually undeservedly, by someone other than the one to whom it seems to belong; but, and most importantly, all this does not remove the responsibility from anyone for being human, for being God's creature in his world. It is a means of enabling such life to emerge, where previously it has been obscured or repressed. Rooted in the realities of human life and behaviour and their unconscious aspects, this atonement genuinely offers salvation. Change, or conversion, does not require us first to deny what we are – human beings made in the image of God, with the authority to act and the need to co-operate with him and one another.

The atonement can thus be interpreted congruently with its tradition as a key Christian doctrine and integrated with the demands of contemporary life and experience. Much modern theological writing on the cross is devoted to the history of the doctrine or treats the atonement as a subdivision of the incarnation. The danger in such stances is that the debate steadily moves away from the arena of everyday belief and unbelief. Even doxological theology, which takes as its ground the Christian experience and tradition of worship, seems to leave a large gap around the atonement, preferring to approach the person and significance of Christ by other routes. Yet the cross is the distinctive symbol of Christianity, and it is to the cross that Christian faith continually turns in practice, not least in the two sacraments of baptism (buried with Christ) and Eucharist ('Do this in remembrance of me'). It is, therefore, vital for Christian belief and practice that a way of integrating the cross with current appreciations of common human experience be found, if the gospel is to continue to commend itself.

CHAPTER THREE

Working vulnerability: the atonement and pastoral care

The atonement is rightly judged by how effective it is in bringing salvation to men and women. This has often been described in terms of benefits received. Through his death Christ earns benefits for mankind – eternal life, a new way of living, an intimate relationship with God, or release from the burden and consequences of sin. But we are less confident about motivation than our predecessors and are acutely sensitive in personal and pastoral relationships to the question. 'For whose benefit is this work actually being done? Is it genuinely for the "client", or is the minister or counsellor constructing and enjoying an "ego-trip"?'

RELATIONSHIPS

A doctrine of the atonement today has to be less concerned with benefit than with involvement. Relationships raise questions of whether we can trust ourselves to one another. The experience of salvation in this setting is what we can only describe as being taken into the mystery of God. This may sound insufficiently down-to-earth and so cause us to hesitate because of the obvious connection between mystery, mysticism and fantasy. But the more we examine the cross from the major perspective of our age (namely our awareness of our own human behaviour), the more we see it as an invitation to encounter God and the transcendent dimension of life at hitherto unperceived depths. He is not, as it were, laid out on a couch for us to examine. That is not the vulnerability of the cross. It is that God exercises his responsibility for creation, for mankind, but above all, for himself as he publicly accepts the consequences. Such action does not add something to what we already are. Rather, by being invited to peer through the window of the cross, we are freed from any need to assume a role

– saint or sinner, dependent or autonomous – in order to contact God. He invites us here to acknowledge the one role that we have been assigned by virtue of our creation – human beings. None have to transform themselves before the cross can transform them.

TRANSGRESSION

Pastoring is sometimes described as 'a ministry of reconciliation'. The phrase is grand and has Pauline authority, but is sometimes weak in content. It drifts into a bland wish that personal relations in a family or communication within an organization should get better. Drawing people together becomes an end in itself. But this lacks rigour; there is no clear purpose; ambivalence and ambiguity are discounted, and (though much is justified) little is achieved. But achievement lies at the root of the atonement. Pastoral practice informed by this doctrine is likely to be purposeful.

The vague sense of reconciliation arises when we underestimate transgression. Anselm's judgement remains apposite to many views of God's action in the incarnation and atonement: 'You have not yet taken sufficient account of the significance of sin.' 'Transgression' is a rich word, making explicit the sense of movement that is implicit in every notion of sin. When these notions become codified, the pastor loses contact with human reality. But when transgression is seen as movement, the underlying ambiguities and ambivalences, which are the condition for atonement, emerge.

NECESSARY TRANSGRESSION

People need to transgress, first to live and subsequently to develop. Our earliest move may be away from assumptions about our mother. Later we embark on adventures, some of which pay off and some of which do not. The first drink or the first kiss can open the way to responsible flowering as a growing adult or be the first step on the road to perdition. Christian moralists have sometimes claimed to be surer of the direction of that step than is possible. Every such experiment is ambiguous and stirs up ambivalence in us.

These moves also involve violence. This may appear as a rejection of our upbringing as we challenge home and parental influence. Or it may be seen as an attack on the accepted ideas and principles by which we have hitherto lived. We then become personally disturbed and unsure of ourselves. Such aggression, towards ourselves or others, is nevertheless essential, since without this type of fight we do not become anything at all. The pastor regularly meets both types of person: those who have committed some transgression and are anxious about having done it and about its consequences; and those who need to transgress but are equally unsure in themselves and anxious about doing so.

Transgression is bound up with ambivalence and the ambiguity of our world. It is also connected with action, cost and achievement – all characteristics of the atonement. Simply, therefore, to invoke the notion of reconciliation devalues the feelings of violence that need to be acknowledged when we are dealing with transgression. The pastor also needs to realize that in dealing with sin he is handling a state of mind that lies deep in feelings and often beyond words. Eventually such feelings may be articulated, but we need first to recognize that they are basically pre-verbal.

Example: Jesus' early ministry

An illustration of this dimension to ministry is found in the initial stories of Jesus in Mark's Gospel. As soon as Jesus is fully into his role as healer and teacher, conflicts arise with the leaders of the prevailing culture as he heals a leper, plucks corn on the sabbath, cures the man with a withered hand and is finally accused of being the devil's agent. Jesus boldly transgresses: by reinterpreting the bonds of convention, which stifle people's freedom, he effectively breaks them.

But there is a second underlying theme. The stories also make the point that these controversies are mostly pre-verbal. The participants do not seem to engage with each other, and the arguments have a tangential quality, which forebodes worse to come. We are, however, left in little doubt that both Jesus and his opponents feel strongly about the issues which are raised. Under the surface lies imminent violence. Anger is explicit in Mark 3.5. Mark 1.41: 'felt compassion' has 'was angry' as an alternative (Greek version). Feeling is so strong that, at least at the start of his ministry, Jesus and those with whom he deals lack suitable categories or language through which to express themselves.

RECONCILIATION

In this setting reconciliation is not the resolution of conflict or the recovery of a happier state of affairs. That would merely be to restore an existing constraint from which the person concerned is emerging with a struggle. There is a necessary anxiety about living which the pastor cannot and should not try to diminish. The cross and atonement as the model for his work affirms the fight/flight dynamic of human life and its characteristic of addressing ambivalence and producing anxiety. It is not Christian ministry, nor any form of reconciliation, to minimize this aspect of life.

The atonement assigns central significance to feelings. Christians are often taught to be wary of feelings, and with some justification. But there is a difference between feelings as emotion and feelings as an aspect of the individual which is not easily articulated. This is the point of the pastor's involvement with sin or transgression, although the tradition of hearing confession and offering spoken counsel may obscure this. But this ministry, when rooted in a dynamic sense of transgression, both conforms to the theological model of the atonement and brings opportunity of salvation to individuals.

THE HOLDING ENVIRONMENT

A useful concept for understanding this ministry is 'the holding environment'. Emotionally deprived people need a setting which is designed to contain their feelings of anger and apathy, aggression and disinterest. Doctors, nurses, therapists and other workers do not provide this; it is negotiated in interaction with the patients as they respond to them in an assured, and therefore reassuring, fashion. Security that was hitherto missing is thus created, and treatment can begin.

The ministry of confession and absolution is similar. The priest and penitent, by meeting within particular constraints of time, place and formality, contract to create a temporary holding environment. In this the unsayable may be said and both have permission to articulate what is usually unspoken, even to oneself. But as the penitent speaks, he or she not only tells the priest of remembered sins and negligences; taking part in the process also involves reordering the penitent's internal world, just as negotiating the holding environment is part of the patient's treatment.

The priest, therefore, even in this most priestly of ministries, is conforming to the pattern of ministry based upon the way of the cross. She is used – in the sense that the penitent makes what he or she will of her. This determines, for example, the form that the confession takes. The priest does not prescribe this, in spite of formularies. Indeed, the sensitive priest has to be prepared for things not to be what they seem: the penitent may talk in an allusive fashion; requests for advice may be expressions of immature, and inappropriate, dependence; self-assertion may be disguised as repentance.

The priest's counsel and, when required, judgement in response to the confession is interpretative. It may seem more directive than this, especially if penances are involved. But interpretation is not the priest giving answers; it is a function of the encounter itself, and so is a joint effort by the two concerned.

Absolution, within this scheme, has a twofold function. In terms of transgression, it first clarifies the form that the sinner's transgressions have hitherto taken within the ambiguities of life and the ambivalence of our human nature. I heard a layperson once comment in discussion: 'You clergy will not get anywhere with us until you realize that, while you talk about black and white, all our life is lived in grey.' Second, and paradoxically, absolution gives permission to transgress in the other sense of the term – to grow by risk. As we saw in thinking about the atonement, forgiveness is not the result of confession; it is the precondition. Although this is not necessarily the frame of mind with which the penitent comes, it is vital that it is the priest's framework of reference.

PASTORING AND PROJECTION

In everyday life projection is often involved in the push for achievement. Those engaged in a struggle, for example, and eager to succeed in some course of action, are notoriously prone to misjudge reality. In their oversimplified world they rush towards their goal, real or imagined, headlong and careless of everything and everyone. By preventing us from seeing that what we are attacking is partly ourselves, projection can be a temporary way of alleviating stress, but only at cost to all concerned. The unconscious process brings relief to the person who is doing the projecting, and simultaneously stirs up emotions in the recipient. The more violent the projection, the more likely it is that the response will be similarly marked. Caught in a cycle, people find themselves becoming increasingly irrational.

But projection is not a ploy that we occasionally bring out of our psychic cupboard. As we have seen, projection is a basic ingredient in normal human behaviour, and consequently in pastoral ministry. It is found in every relationship, and that of the pastor with the penitent is not immune. Ministerial expertise, therefore, is to follow the model of the atonement and transform what is inhibiting or potentially destructive to new creativity. When we realize that projection constitutes basic human behaviour and is not a weakness or failure, we can seek ways of employing it in the service of pastoral ministry.

Projective behaviour and the associated feelings, however, are not confined to the individual, as, for example, was the case with the confessional. These dynamics also underlie the activity of the local church as an identifiable part of a particular social context, as the following study demonstrates.

Example: the village with two churches

In a large village parish there were two church buildings with a congregation linked to each. One was the old church; the other a 'new' (nineteenth-century) building. The original reasons why the second church was built were complicated, but by the time of this story the village had largely developed around the newer church. It was in the centre of the largest segment of population, by the shops and adjacent to other amenities. The old church was on the fringe. The vicar was overstretched to provide a full range of services at both churches. In addition the village was not so large that the distances were too great to expect people who wished to worship to travel to the central church. These were points of fact.

But the vicar also believed that public expression of church unity was important as a statement of Christian belief and practice. He set out, therefore, on what he regarded as a ministry of reconciliation, not by closing one church but by fostering a stronger sense of unity in the whole parish and its expression in worship in one centre. He carefully involved the church council in consultation. Although different forms of worship prevailed in each church – the old services at the old church and newer ones at the central building – he was happy with this state of affairs, and indeed encouraged the council to think about how both forms of worship could continue to be provided.

The priest was experienced enough to expect disagreement. But he was unprepared for the irrational outburst that followed. Suddenly, and not only in the church, but also throughout the village, unsuspected divisions emerged. Two camps were established on almost every issue that arose, not just the future of the church buildings. What is more, the members of each camp changed according to the issue. The vicar was bewildered. His previous experience failed him. He found irreconcilable splits developing in him between, for instance, his intentions and actions and his gospel and his practice. He began to reckon that he was the wrong man for the parish and that he should, at cost to himself and his family, immediately move. The situation was suffused with anger, which was expressed at unexpected moments in strange ways. Friends became enemies; colleagues fell out over trivial matters. Irrational behaviour seemed uninterpretable. Sensible, competent people, among them the vicar, could not cope.

In various ways the vicar was made to feel that he was the cause of the problem. He first interpreted what was happening in terms of projections from all the parties directly into him. But after consultation a different perspective opened up. On examination it appeared that the hitherto uncontentious issue of two churches in a small village had long been used to contain many differences and arguments so that they remained unexpressed. Now, however, because the two churches themselves had been made the centre of attention, they could no longer function in this fashion in people's unconscious worlds. Consequently disarray prevailed and the vicar was a convenient focal point for people's ambivalences. He was a repository for the strong antipathies that different groups could not express to each other.

This behaviour was primitive, in that people found powerful but ambiguous feelings aroused in themselves. On the one hand they wished to get at each other and formed odd alliances to achieve this; on the other hand they longed to avoid any engagement. They were caught in fight/flight. All felt that they were struggling to achieve something important, but without any awareness that everybody's 'something' was insubstantial – their own needs. The vicar, who had inadvertently exposed these raw feelings, found that people displaced their anxieties and anger, together with their ambiguity and ambivalence, into the church leadership, chiefly him.

This is a simple instance of the corporate use of projection as a defence. Originally it had been against examining differences of self-awareness and intention in the church. This was conveniently provided by the existence of the two buildings. Each was being used by all concerned, not just by those who attended, to contain their uncertainties. In both congregations, for example, one group was concerned about the old services and another about the new. This struggle, familiar in any church, was in this case mainly avoided at the level of feeling by allowing one group to represent conservatism and the other innovation. Whether this was true or not remained unexamined. In fact each congregation included members with different views. It was easier, however, to project such ambivalence into the other congregation than to be responsible for a definite position within one's own.

When, having inadvertently removed this framework, the vicar began to promote the idea of reconciliation in the guise of a united fellowship of Christians, he, again unwittingly, created a nugatory focus for people's feelings. Christian fellowship, itself an ideal, was in this context nothing more than a fantasy. One reason was that the congregations were reflecting more than their internal dilemmas. There were also powerful divisions within the developing village community, in particular whether it was to hold on to its old image of itself or creatively to develop a new one. This idea of fellowship, therefore, sounded plausible, but proved insubstantial. Everyone's dilemma became worse. The ambivalence in the village as a whole was being projected into the different aspects of church life and contributing to its ambiguity; but these facets of church life themselves were being focused in something which all knew and felt to be unreal – idealized Christian fellowship.

Atonement applied

The situation may appear irredeemable. At this point, however, it became possible to act on the model of the atonement and to see how it could enable a Christian congregation to find God in these ambiguities and prevailing projections, and so deal with them realistically (in terms of its organization) and spiritually (in terms of its developing Christian life).

First, the vicar recognized that he had misinterpreted the situation, with hindsight almost inevitably. As leader of the church and as the focus of so much of the confusion, he had to surrender parts of himself, chiefly his ideal of a united church. This cleared the ground so that the projections that people were employing could be exposed. A further reality was also affirmed: there was no question in the vicar's mind of closing a church. This was in practice reinforced by the diocesan authorities, who, anticipating local developments, were not prepared to dispose of the building.

Second, a consistent stance was adopted. Every group, however important or apparently unimportant, was encouraged in its meetings to examine its internal divisions and was carefully dissuaded from the simple device of projecting them outwards. Thus they found themselves having to ask why such things mattered to them and so to take back what hitherto they had angrily disposed of into others. The same question was always asked as to why it mattered both to them in their role or through them to the constituency that they represented. Here aspects of the way of the cross became explicit: representation and responsibility, as well as self-surrender in the interests of a greater task. They were not made to feel guilty for having used others. There would have been no future in that; any such sense was a spin-off, not a central concern. They were, however, deliberately asked to examine their own feelings and beliefs.

Third, the exercise was set in a wider context than that which people usually employed. In the cross the political and social factors which coincided are important but not ultimately central. Jesus' death tests everything, and to do that has to be specifically set among questions about the nature of God himself. In this case, if discussion had been by church people in the context of church life alone, it might have been instructive but probably not effective. The notion of a whole church, which had been used, had proved an illusion. So church people were invited to try and think about what was happening to them in the setting of the village community as a whole, of which they were also members. It soon became apparent that the congregations were colluding with the village as a whole in ignoring a third area. The village included a housing estate, which was unconnected with either church or with either end of the village. It was marginal in every way. The village community and the church seemed to be dividing over comparatively unimportant issues so as not to have to address a major reality about the village – how this housing estate was to be incorporated into its life.

This process involved cost. The vicar had to abandon ideas which were dear to him. The congregations and groups within them had to undergo the pain of repentance and change. The effort of thinking in the way described also carried a cost.

Inevitably, therefore, a few individuals could not endure and left. But by now most members of the congregation and the vicar were sufficiently sensitized to projection that they were able, so far as they could, to avoid allowing these few to carry off unresolved feelings of anger and disarray. This work was evidenced by the fact that to everyone's surprise so small a number left. The tensions of ministry in the village remain, and the divisions are not magically healed or reconciled. But the change now is that because they can be acknowledged they can be explored, interpreted and used. The basic dynamic remains; but it is now harnessed to a task of ministry rather than given expression through the idealized notion of fellowship.

THE PASTOR'S ROLE

The role of the pastor is, as we have noted, a function of the task of the church in its context. When people approach a minister for care, absolution or advice, whatever their stated wish, they are approaching a publicly religious figure and so addressing something which that role represents to them, whether they consciously realize this or not. The minister may experience this as affirming or denying. We receive a variety of projections, usually at the same time. They need disentangling. The key to this unravelling lies in focusing on feelings that are confusingly aroused in us. We should not expect them to be otherwise. People bring with them ideas about God and religion that are not likely to be sophisticated and articulate but primitive and incapable of being spoken.

Nevertheless the model of the atonement undergirds and emphasizes how important is this phase of pastoral ministry. Through the cross God himself accepts and interprets the fantasies that are projected on to him, specifically the dependent fantasy that magic can in the end be expected. What does it mean for men and women and God himself that the offered saviour does not perform the ultimate miracle?

There [i.e. on the cross] above all and for the last time the miracle did not take place. 'Let the Christ, the King of Israel, come down now from the cross, that we may see and believe' (Mark 15.32), they shout. And they kept on shouting while he perished in misery. And the miracle, boldly demanded, secretly expected, devoutly hoped for, ardently prayed for, did not take place.[1]

This is the issue, however, with which in the Gospel stories Jesus himself first has to struggle. He has to live with and acknowledge his own feelings, which are profoundly affected by the contradictory projections of his disciples and the crowd, in order to be able to interpret these back to them. The cost of that interpretation in this case was the crucifixion. But because he offers back interpreted projections at this ultimate cost to himself, others are eventually able to struggle with the nature of their own belief.

This is the cross as the basis of pastoral ministry. First, we realize that projections, although they stir up powerful feelings, are chiefly directed to the minister's roles. Second, we discover that opportunities for interpretative ministry arise as we accept these roles and the associated projections and, exploring the feelings generated in us, use them as the basis for our response to people. Thus the Christian story becomes gospel – good news. It is generated as we respond to people's assumptions about us as God's representatives with our life and corresponding interpretative stance informed by Scripture, tradition and faith. Third, this position holds us, in the face of pressure to adopt other stances that are sometimes more congruent with the assumptions of the age or with our own self-image, to our priestly role as the significant point of address.[2] In so doing we shall not confuse, for example, penitents by treating them as clients, or normal souls seeking ministry by treating them as neurotic.

GUILT AND FORGIVENESS

As a presumed 'God person', the pastor will inevitably at some time be invited to deal with guilt and forgiveness. Indeed these are probably lurking somewhere on the agenda of most people who approach her. This is an area where clarity is important.

Guilt may be a form of fear and anxiety which, through a personality disorder, becomes morbid. The Church has sometimes made a speciality of this, inducing it in order to absolve it. But there is also a proper sense of guilt, of which the penitent can be aware and so forgiven. This sort of guilt, which is self-engendered, is less widely recognized today, since the notion of guilt as a form of disorder tends to dominate popular thought.

The pastor needs to understand that guilt is not necessarily a condition but a set of feelings arising from the basic ambiguity and ambivalence of the human condition. Guilt, therefore, is also endemic and cannot be casually removed or explained. But these two facets – the morbid and the proper – are also intertwined. When dealing with someone feeling guilty we are touching primitive parts of their deepest self. Such guilt, therefore, will not be lightly removed by absolution nor can it be ritually abolished. The pastor first needs discernment.

Guilt arises from feelings of being crushed in our interactions. These are with other people, with our own inner worlds or more generally with the context in which we live. This is why guilty feelings are difficult to locate. The experience is of being caught both ways.

Example: slavery

Over the centuries Christians have been confused on the issue of slavery, which now seems clear. Here all three interactions, with others, with ourselves and with our context, come together. The earliest Christians seem to have been unaware that slavery might be an evil. They displayed little, if any, guilt for what was done to fellow human beings and were devoid of feelings. As, however, awareness grew, people began to feel guilty and many, finally most, shifted from their indifference as these feelings were interpreted, the complexity of their guilt was eventually perceived and absolution followed action – the freeing of slaves.

But guilt has a double edge: on the one hand we feel guilt for our ignorance in not noticing that anything is wrong; on the other hand there is also guilt for our knowledge, when that comes about. We are crushed in a pincer movement between ignorance and knowledge and between ourselves and our external world, from which there seems no escape. We participate in a world that we do not necessarily enjoy but which also orders our ways of participating.

Forgiveness, therefore, would not be release from that guilt, since it would become release from the world. Flight of this kind is uncreative and leads to religion being a delusion. The first stage to forgiveness is to allow people their ambivalence and to acknowledge it. This sounds dully conformist, but it is, as the cross shows, the first step towards salvation:

It is all this that Christian traditions invite us to celebrate in the sacrament of forgiveness: tensions, conflicts, transgressions, prophetic words or actions, the confession of new sins, the request for forgiveness, and the acceptance of forgiveness accorded.[3]

This guilt is a basic human condition which needs to be affirmed as the first step to forgiveness, absolution and the recovering of responsibility. The minister bases this affirmation on his grasp of the cross of Christ. He can then go further.

Forgiveness does not free us from the guilt which is a dimension of our humanity; it is transformed from being destructive to creative. The popular belief that to forgive is to forget is seriously at fault when we recognize that men and women are responsible beings with conscious and unconscious worlds. Where deep feelings, whatever their origin, are concerned, forgetfulness is impossible. They and their origins may be consciously forgotten, but they remain in our unconscious mind and may later emerge, much to everyone's surprise. The secret of forgiveness is remembrance, to rehearse the past so as to acknowledge it as ours.

The Christian proclamation of forgiveness through the cross of Christ makes precisely this point. The historical moment of crucifixion becomes the turning point in Christian teaching. Remembrance becomes a way of living. Whatever else may be lost, dismissed or fantasized away, there is no gospel without recourse to at least one historical reality – a crucifixion. Even when this remembrance is ritualized in worship, it still refers to a specific moment. The eucharistic canon itself holds the cross at the centre of the Church's worship, where the worshippers 'show forth the Lord's death' (1 Corinthians 11.26). And from earliest times the creeds included the phrase 'under Pontius Pilate' to root salvation in history. So Rufinus in the fourth century remarks:

> Those who handed down the creed showed great wisdom in underlining the actual date at which these things happened, so that there might be no chance of any uncertainty or vagueness upsetting the stability of the tradition.[4]

A vital ingredient in any ministry modelled on the atonement is a similar emphasis on detail. It reminds the minister that all interpretation, even of the vast issues of human life and meaning, has to be focused, not just in a general sense on the person concerned but also specifically through the minister's actual feelings in that particular encounter. He is consistently pulled back from the world of fantasies to what is here and now, what can be recalled.

Undergirding the pastoral response to guilt and forgiveness are two further facets of the atonement. The first is the familiar one of unconditional acceptance and grace. Here a grasp of morbid and proper guilt is essential. A major problem with people who feel acute guilt is that they cannot accept themselves. It is no use speaking to them of the accepting grace of God, since they have insufficient sense of their self to which to apply it. The pastor needs the model of the atonement to work with rather than any easy assumption about its benefits. His role is to embody this acceptance by willingly receiving projections on behalf of God before attempting to offer them back in interpretation. Held thus, those with guilty souls are given space and assurance to discover to what extent they might become able to accept themselves.

In this consideration of guilt and the pastor's dealing with it we are in a larger field than that of formal confession and absolution. We have previously seen how that occupies a negotiated setting, in which there are reasonably defined roles: priest, with authority to hear confession and offer absolution, and penitent, in the role of one seeking formal forgiveness. These public roles may obscure several others which are covertly assumed, but they are the basis of the encounter. Here, however, we are considering the overwhelming, generalized role that the minister may possess by virtue of being regarded as 'the God-person'.

Pastors are thus foci for a range of projections, and taking these is a thankless task. But the cross sustains the pastor, where God demonstrates that it is his way of working to hold projections and sustain them against every pressure to discount or dismiss them. Even when, therefore, projection from a penitent on to him as a representative of God becomes acute, the minister knows that he is not being asked to be something other than he is or to handle the impossible. He has his given model as the basic notion by which to sustain his ministry.

In the Christian tradition forgiveness is confirmed by action. Forgiveness is not a feeling or a state but an experience that is demonstrated in action. By this means the orientation towards achievement, which is the mark of the fight/flight dynamic that underlies the atonement, is preserved. The action chiefly possesses symbolic significance, since it will always be inadequate.

But it reminds the penitent, the pastor and others that reconciliation is neither easy nor ever complete. Because it always
includes potential change, it has a forward look to it and must
remain open to new possibilities.

The cross is concerned with achievement and hopeful possibilities of change and newness. Forgiveness of the past implies
future action based upon that past. That is why any notion of
eradicating that past is theologically, pastorally and psychologically false. Forgiveness is not losing what has been acquired,
however debased it may on reflection seem, and even if it is a
cause for guilt. Whatever guilt may desire, absolution recovers
and revalues some formative experiences or behaviour, which will
not and cannot be lost. They remain, but they no longer need
crush.

EVANGELISM AND THE CROSS

Today's churches and ministers are worried about the churches'
evangelistic task. The doctrine of the atonement is the heart of
the gospel proclamation, and St Paul defines it: 'We preach Christ
crucified' (1 Corinthians 1.23). The evangelist, like the pastor, is
called to embody Christ, so that through him people may uncover
some of their projections. The proclamation, therefore, is of
Christ's cross as the way which all are invited to follow. It is not
composed of assured consequences which some may have derived
for themselves from meditation upon that way.

In the light of our present discussion, we can regard evangelism as mobilizing fight. It is essentially an aggressive stance,
emphasizing that the proclaimer has a message to impart to
others. In this sense, therefore, it is similar to marketing in its
demand for behaviour that is orientated towards achievement.
Yet, as we have seen, this dynamic is the one most prone to sup-
porting fantasies and delusion about oneself, about others and
about the message. To be effective, a fight has to be at the right
time, in the right place, and about the right issue.

This way of the cross is marked by that integrity which persistently faces reality and lives with it. It speaks of affirmed
ambivalence and ambiguity; of the cost of achievement; of the
demands of personal integrity; and of effective living on behalf
of others. These are the evangelistic themes that are illuminated by the powerful story of the crucifixion. To be saving they

have specifically to address the person hearing rather than express a particular doctrine.

Most forms of evangelism have at some time been criticized as indulging in projection. But this accusation is no reason for special anxiety. All human interactions, as we have seen, are to some extent projective. The test of the evangelist, which itself derives from the cross he proclaims, is what is done with those projections, both those that he receives and, more importantly, his upon the hearers. The clue to this, and to evangelism today, lies in the notion of the witness.

The Christian witness does not say his piece on every occasion; he embodies what he proclaims even to death, if needs be, as martyr.[5] Evangelism, therefore, is not just preaching, with the attendant risk of the evangelist merely projecting into his audience. It must include somewhere in its process the struggle to interpret projections, received and given. Like Christ, a person who claims to speak the word of God should expect to deal with projections that people believe that they cannot effectively direct to God himself. They are thrown at God through the evangelist, and so become for him both primary data about the people he is addressing and simultaneously data for creating God's word in that context. It seems unlikely, therefore, that evangelism can take place according to the model of the cross without personal engagement, or, at least, a context which fosters that sense in those being addressed. This question needs further thought in our world of media saturation and new forms of communication, in so far as they may implicitly encourage the belief that personal engagement may be less important than the mere presentation of the message.

The supposed conflict between pastoring and evangelizing is another instance of that defensive splitting and projection that marks our human lives, and it too stands under the judgement of the cross. Aggressive connotations to the gospel, however, do need to be recognized, not just in terms of how the Christian addresses his own feelings of anger and rage, but also when we ask how they can be mobilized to create activity on the part of the people of God. We are, therefore, now at the point to consider which aspect of our personal religious life is addressed by the atonement.

CHAPTER FOUR

Taking up your cross: atonement and the disciples' spirituality

The path of discipleship is the way of spirituality – and that word is over-used. Churches hold working parties and recruit committees, organize discussion groups and train spiritual directors in order to discover its content. Some problems with the idea arise because the word changes its meaning at different moments in the Church's history. So when we are pointed to the so-called 'spiritual classics', we find that the writers are not quite dealing with our questions. The term oscillates between the private concern and preoccupation with religious activity and a way of viewing and informing the whole of life. 'Spiritual', for example, has referred to the religious life of the clergy by contrast with the temporal possessions and activities of the Church. The spiritual life is always in danger of being restricted to higher or, so it is believed, more important areas than those in which most human beings live. But at its best, spirituality concerns the meaning of everyday life. It speaks of a life informed by and responding to belief in the transcendent, God. The term describes the profound quality of ordinary human life, and because of that it presses a fundamental ambivalence on those who would be spiritual. They constantly have to ask whether they find themselves in a particular situation because they are human beings or because they are Christian disciples.

This is a false antithesis, but one that nonetheless frequently emerges in confessions and discussions. However unreal in theory, it is a division that is felt in practice. It, therefore, cannot be removed by theological rationale but has to be faced as a phenomenon of human and religious life. For example, God must ultimately be and remain unknowable. This belief, however, does not derive solely from the problems of knowing God – his essential hiddenness. It is part of our ambivalence in the face of those factors which, like God, enlarge the dimensions within which we live. We want them but fear them. In the tradition of the dark night of the soul, for example, we discover a sense of the hidden God at the same time as we are faced with our blinded soul's unwillingness to see his light. It is neither one nor the other, but both.

DISCIPLESHIP AND THE CROSS

Christian discipleship is marked by the same characteristics as the cross: ambivalence in ourselves; ambiguity in our context; the need for decision and action; and the question of cost. These are also, as we have noted, marks of common human experience. Some forms of discipleship may seem to be superimposed on everyday life. But discipleship is not about benefits and additions and there is no future in this approach for the Christian way of life. Christian spirituality is not about additives but catalysts. It is the human journey lived in the illumination and under the judgement of the way of the cross. It is, therefore, a way of discomfort, not because of any morbid wish pathologically to identify ourselves with the suffering Christ, but because it affirms the ambivalence and ambiguity in our human condition.

SPIRITUALITY AND AMBIVALENCE

We have seen how ambivalence is a state in our development that is built upon the profound anxiety of our earliest life. Ambivalence, therefore, itself is ambiguous: it is an achievement, but one which is always questioned. It persists as does doubt. The dependence which characterizes religious belief makes doubt appear a reprehensible form of unfaithfulness. But doubt is essential. If we are not uncertain about ourselves, our decisions, our world, or our meaning, then we are not open to the options available to us. We have implicitly closed some down. Doubt is best thought of as 'valued ambivalence'. This gives us a chance to be creative, because it alerts us to the potential for change when we engage both our inner world and our context.

This human feeling represents everyone's potential as a child of God. The complexities of life are such that we sometimes feel that to survive we need to become more sure about ourselves and our place within the world. But feeling doubtful about this, we excuse ourselves and propel ourselves into guilt. This type of guilt is appropriate to human beings; it can be forgiven by confirming that the ambivalent feelings, which have generated it, are desirable because they arise from what we all are – creatures in God's creation.

The central Christian teaching on this, which is embodied in the death of Jesus, is that the way of discipleship is that of forgiveness, particularly of those whom we perceive as enemies. This goes to the heart of changing oneself, and changing the world, because it simultaneously brings about three effects, each of which offers hope.

First, we take back the negative aspects of ourselves which contribute to our definition of 'enemy'. The stronger the feeling of hostility towards someone, however seemingly justified, the more it includes aspects of ourselves. Change here first requires honesty. Facing this and so taking back as best we may our projections, we are changed.

Second, by doing this we actually affect the 'enemy'. As projection is recognized and withdrawn, his feelings are also altered. Whatever the causes of his hostility – and this does not pretend to be a total explanation – he will at least be freed from responding to projections from us which he probably does not understand but which he certainly feels. The free, or forgiven, person brings hope to others.

Third, the relationship itself is adjusted. We are not, therefore, in speaking of forgiveness merely outlining an approach to person-to-person relationships. We are also talking about a fundamental change in the structures within which they are locked and the interrelation between them, a discernible shift in an otherwise blocked world. The way of discipleship is to embody affirmed, redeemed and so creative ambivalence.

The other mark of this way is curiosity. One indicator of a delinquent family is the absence of curiosity on the part of its members about one another. But in the arena of faith the effect of ambivalence is to encourage curiosity. So once again we see that something which is often considered by religious people a negative – doubt – in fact is a desirable state of faith, since the doubter is consistently and constantly curious. The classic story of this, of course, is Thomas, who doubts the resurrection until he can bring his curiosity to bear and his questions are answered. But once he has done that, his commitment is complete and he does not need to accept the invitation to touch Jesus' risen body itself.

The ambivalence within us is matched by the ambiguity of our context as we experience it. We know that we are bound up in a network of relationships and institutions, some of which we dimly perceive and most of which lie beyond our comprehension. Every specific context, when given our attention, becomes ambiguous. When we think we may have sorted ourselves out, the world confuses us. The core of Christian spirituality, however, is not a private affair of survival within the chaos; it is concerned with social involvement – that is, being part of the human race and the created order.

Example: ecumenical striving

It is important, however, that we acknowledge how inherently ambiguous all human life is. One consequence of failing to grasp this may be seen in a contemporary issue of discipleship – the disagreements between Christian churches, which seem increasingly inappropriate in today's world. Indeed, the grounds for disagreement become more complex as our society develops. Ecumenical striving has been, and is, an attempt to remove such discord. The twentieth century was a time when ecumenical endeavour possibly reached an all-time high. At times it was a great hope, although possibly the greatest Christian event was not open to all the churches, although all the churches have been affected by it. This was the Second Vatican Council, with which the Roman Catholic Church is still coming to terms.

But it has become increasingly clear that the hope that one outcome would be ecumenical work together, noble as it is, is hopelessly misplaced. For dissension is not solely grounded in church structures and ancient or modern disputes. These contribute, but largely as vehicles for our difficulties in dealing with our human context. As units in their social setting churches participate as much as any other bodies in the prevailing confusions of the world. But they incorporate these into a confined space of belief and religious practice. There, so it is believed, profound dissension can be effectively understood.

But by thinking in terms of 'understanding', Christians casually translate contemporary difficulty into historical terms. They then produce the customary ecumenical document: almost certainly study of some scripture, a worthy statement of intent, a long historical excursus, and usually brief proposals for action. Since these, however, chiefly derive from the historical excursus rather than from the realities of present-day experiences of disciples, they are difficult to implement. In this way, however, we convince ourselves that we can avoid the problems of living with the ambiguity of religious belief. For this finds expression in the existence of different churches, and with the social dynamics which lead to distinctive expectations being focused in these separate churches by the communities in which they are set. But we pretend that the problems of living originate from profound doctrinal differences.

These are genuine concerns for Christian discipleship and spiritual growth. Yet we need to recognize that the underlying factor is more immediate than we sometimes realize. It is the ambiguity of our context, because this, too, the cross endorses as more than an unfortunate problem. Every setting in which something has to be done includes possibilities of success and failure. The cross itself is a specific paradigm of this at one point in history.

This ambiguity and uncertainty mobilizes fight/flight, the dynamic which, as we saw earlier, is stimulated from our earliest moments by our increasingly coming to terms with our outside world. In other words, the ambiguity of the world is not something to be endured; it is to be accepted and enjoyed as what enables us to exist at all. Under stress we may curse the world and blame God for allowing it to be as it is. From this dilemma, however, as Job discovered, spiritual maturity will not allow us so comfortable an escape. His story is confirmed in the Christian spiritual tradition based on the way of the cross, a way of engagement, risk, error and forgiveness.

SPIRITUALITY AND ACTION

When we have taken into account ambivalence and ambiguity, there remains the need to do something. If deciding is problematic, acting is more so. Yet action is intrinsic to Christian spirituality. There are no passive individuals or groups either on or around the cross. Each has a decision to make and an action consequent upon it. Similarly with the Christian way: action is necessary, and decisions without action are void. That is why mission and evangelism are bound up with Christian spirituality, and without them spirituality is a debased concept.

To emphasize the significance of action for spirituality is not to conform to the ideas of success which prevail in our frenetic

world. This dismal form of spiritual teaching is sometimes proclaimed in the name of Christ. Yet it is not based on the realities
of the atonement but on collusion between the teacher and the
audience's dependent longings which render them gullible.
When this happens religion again proves a delusion. Yet action,
as a basic ingredient of the pattern of the cross, provides the
critical norm for Christian decision-making. Disciples act in
such a fashion as to become available and vulnerable to the
scrutiny of others. Like Christ, they become a window through
which people can gain a glimpse of a depth in their being, which
is God. Or, we might say more traditionally, they become Christ
to their neighbour.

Luther's bold exhortation in his letter to Melanchthon in 1556,
'Be a sinner and sin strongly, but more strongly have faith and
rejoice in Christ,' captures this vision.[1] Similarly the Christian is
continually exhorted to act decisively, not in order to test God but
to become accessible to others for their scrutiny. Without the risk
of action Christians cease to be identifiable, the gospel becomes
shrouded, and spiritual life will become introverted as mission
declines.

There are today, as ever, deep divisions over what constitutes
Christian action. Social and political activity is so rife in society
that a distinctive Christian contribution is difficult to determine.
The cross, however, provides some indicators for the activity of
discipleship. First, because it is set in a historical context and
represents not only actions between God and his world but
between God and himself, it suggests that action based on this
model is collaborative. This word has recently been applied to
shared activity between laity and ordained ministers in the
phrase 'collaborative ministry'. The disciples' spirituality based
on the atonement will not be particularly distinguished by this. It
will, however, be marked by the only collaboration that matters –
that between Christians and others – because in this meeting
Christ himself is found.

Second, the hazard of the cross reminds Christians that, contrary to their deep-felt instincts derived from a sense of thank-
fulness and awe, God does not need their protection. Any action is
risky, especially if it involves someone else's name, not least
God's. But the model of the way of the cross provides a critical test
of action. The question is not only 'Is it shared?', but also 'Has it
been and will it continue to be scrutinized?' and 'Will our activity
encourage this stance in others, whatever their belief?'

What Christians do, therefore, is important, although it may be exactly what others are also doing. The distinctive mark of Christian spirituality is the way in which these actions are consciously used to allow, and encourage, scrutiny by others and the vulnerability that follows. Here we come to the final issue – that of cost.

SPIRITUALITY AND COST

When we act on behalf of others and are used by them, wittingly and unwittingly, cost becomes important. There are bound to be mistakes and hurts with their consequent feelings. And when feelings are rife, blame – apportionment of cost – erupts. Blame and recrimination follow error. Such costs can be absorbed, often without too much difficulty, because when something goes wrong it does not always require much virtue from people to accept that they were involved. There is nothing specially Christian about this or about the fights that are sometimes engendered. On the question of such everyday costs Christians are called to be an example. They pale into insignificance for disciples of the crucified. In other words, by accepting blame that may not directly belong to them, they can extend an invitation to others to live responsibly in a similar fashion. This is part of the way of the cross – 'When he was reviled, he did not revile in return' (1 Peter 2.23). This aspect of the cross directly connects with common human experience, and anyone, believer or not, can be invited to live responsibly in this fashion.

There is, however, a further type of cost, which is harder to accept. It is a central mark of Christian spirituality enlivened by the cross of Christ. To accept and absorb blame for things for which we are not responsible is a dangerous enterprise. It can lead to patronizing others, the pathology of omnipotence and that eagerness to placate everyone which sometimes marks so-called 'Christian' behaviour. Yet bearing costs on behalf of others is Christlike and lies deep in the disciple's spirituality. As with God's work in Christ, the aim is not to relieve others of their responsibilities. The delicate task is to hold responsibility for what does not belong to us so that others may be able to resume or discover their responsibility within God's world. Such self-critical bearing of blame and pain for others is not a permanent state. The skill of the disciple in such ministry is to take up the priestlike task, which is to stand for someone else at a point in their life where, for whatever reason, for the time being they cannot stand. This life on behalf of others is both the stance of Christ and the essence of Christian spirituality.

'On behalf of' is the ultimate clue to the Christian interpretation of life and understanding of God. It, therefore, also informs Christian spirituality and is the point at which the fact of the cross of Christ tests discipleship so that it does not become debased. The little word *hyper* can follow words which cover almost every aspect of discipleship: prayer, working and caring, sacrifice, suffering and dying, and generally being. All the Christian doctrines and the activities rooted in them are in the end tested by the extent that they are testably believed and lived on behalf of others. In the cross, however, we encounter the complete manifestation of this way. God himself demonstrates life devoid of self-interest and wholly lived on behalf of others.

SPIRITUALITY AND SACRAMENTS

Spirituality is sometimes thought of as worship and prayer. But these alone do not involve and convert others. When separated from the critical testing of life, which is the way of discipleship, they become maudlin and self-centred. They lose contact with the awesome reality of a God who works through both the starkness of the cross and the confusions of everyday human existence and are used as escape routes for people in flight. For a while they may be speciously justified as profound trust in God or an intimate relationship with him. But eventually they fail, unless we realize that every experience of faith is only enjoyed vicariously.

This sense of 'on behalf of' is sustained by the story of the cross and by the life lived upon affirmed ambivalence and ambiguity, decisive action, and responsible bearing of cost on behalf of others so that they may take a step further towards becoming responsible human beings. Such is the complex, double dynamic of fight/flight, in which we find robustly functional faith, which brings about change in individuals and in the world – salvation.

There is an interchange between the centre of the Christian faith and human life, which allows Christians to commend the way of the cross as an interpretative tool for living, without first requiring that people believe the Christian message. This stance is confirmed by and permanently enshrined in the two dominical sacraments, each of which is a sacrament of the cross – baptism and Eucharist. But each of these central components of Christian faith and spirituality uses natural symbols – water, wine, bread and oil. Even when Christians attempt to retain them as the prerogative of the believing community – an entry rite and a fellowship meal – they do not lose their wide range of associations. They break out of these confines as people use them. By their nature water and oil, bread and wine can never become the private property of the Christian Church. Thus what Christians most intimately cling to as the focus of their corporate spirituality of the cross turns out to be the property of mankind. Again the particularity of the Christian profession and its universal implication unite.

The cross, Christian spirituality and sacramental thinking coalesce to display divine grace. The Christian gospel finally stands by this statement: you do not have to be a believer to approach God, whether through word or sacrament. Believers, therefore, far from possessing a message from God that they have at all costs to convey to their fellow men and women, are those marked by vulnerability to the scrutiny of their fellow human beings.

The Church has been instinctively right to resist promulgating one orthodox doctrine of the atonement. The power of the cross and the strength of those who walk its way lie in vulnerability, whether to investigation into history or to scrutiny more particularly in the lives of those who profess a Christian spirituality.

CHAPTER FIVE

God saw that it was good: the doctrine of creation

The second doctrine is that of the creation/resurrection. That is a large topic in itself. In addition, the associated dynamic is dependence, which, as we shall again see, is the most pervasive in common human experience. It therefore seemed wise to attend to the new creation specifically alongside the original. For convenience the doctrinal material is subdivided into two: creation and new creation, or resurrection.

THE BASIC DYNAMIC

The dynamic which underlies both creation and resurrection – dependence – permeates human life and is specially prominent when we think of the Church and its gospel From whichever angle we approach this theme – theological, pastoral, in terms of discipleship or from the psychological perspective – it looks massive. The nature of God and the fact of religion join in demanding congruent theological understanding.

But it is also the most down-to-earth belief. Ministers daily deal with this area of human and religious experience. Any better understanding of it, therefore, should illuminate every aspect of church life and ministry, as well the content of the gospel to be proclaimed.

Example: the unbelieving 'believer'

Some years ago I was consulting to a parish priest and as part of getting the 'feel' of the place I was invited to meet a distinguished resident. When I asked what her connection with the local church was, she rapidly distanced herself from it. She did not believe in God or religion; the church authorities were soulless, careless of the beautiful building of which they were custodians; the vicar was at best irrelevant to the life of the town and at worst a malign influence. But when I suggested that logically the church building should be closed and the vicar deployed more usefully elsewhere, she immediately and instinctively responded, 'Oh no! We are our past, and the church is the only guardian of that past. It is a comfort to know that the vicar prays for the town and the world.'

This was a clearer definition than many a churchgoer would manage. The attitude was classically dependent: she wanted a reliable church in order to sustain her beliefs, whatever they were. The powerful pull of dependence is also towards irrationality: the position she adopted of a rationalist was as irrational as anyone could find. This must be taken into account in any attempt to integrate theology and pastoral practice.

The same is true of religion. The phenomenon of religion is inextricably bound up with faith, and will neither go away nor purify itself of its folk accretions and manifestations. Faith, religion and the insistent demand for ritual coincide in worship. This cannot be confined, as sometimes in the contemporary church, to liturgy. We are in a wider field of belief about some being, usually called 'God', who is reckoned to impinge upon us and to whom a response should be made. So with this doctrine we have first to deal with the basic condition of all of life – creation. Then we discuss the distinctively Christian vision of the new creation, the resurrection.

POTENTIAL AND LIMITATION

Behind the statement in the creed that 'We believe in God . . . creator of heaven and earth' lie three affirmations. First, the world, of which we are part and to which we contribute, is what there is and invites interpretation. Because we exist and think objectively and imaginatively about the world, we contribute to its continuing creation. But we do not completely create it. From a psychological perspective people may be said to create their worlds. But for this to happen there must be people to do the creating. There are, therefore, given factors, which we sometimes feel as constraints and which condition what is possible.

Theological responses to this observation vary. But there is no escape from the obvious: there is what there is, however much of this givenness is at any moment undiscovered or unexplored. And this world, the one which we know and not some other, demands that we attempt to interpret it.

The second affirmation is that God comes first. 'God is creator' announces God's freedom, since of his own free will he began it all. It might seem, however, that the modern insight that we create our own worlds contradicts this affirmation. If we remain locked into a simplistic view, this could be the case. But the ability to create our own worlds is a function of our imagination.

In contemporary thought such creativity is being increasingly acknowledged as having a central place: in mathematics and philosophy (for example the work of Michael Polanyi) and in theology and religious studies, such as those by John Bowker. Through imagination we respond to something that is not immediately present in our environment but which we feel is potentially there. We use it to create ideas and imagined worlds. But when we describe this activity we use the language of receiving. Ideas 'strike us', 'come to us', 'occur' and so on. Imaginative activity, then, is a facet of our experience. It is a goal to which we strive but which also appears to come from beyond us. When, therefore, we become aware of our own creative activity, we do not necessarily dispute God's priority.

Third we affirm that God's creation is out of nothing (*ex nihilo*). Out of 'the inner necessity of his love', to use Barth's phrase, the creator makes something that corresponds to him and gives him pleasure.[1] We creatures are finite and mortal because we depend on God for our continued existence. If creation originates in God alone, we can regard the process as purposeful. This purpose is the object of our search for our own creatureliness, leading us to study what there is and who we are. But such belief also implies that God may generate new possibilities and that creation is not limited to what at present is – although that is all that may remain accessible to us – but includes what might be. The danger of such an argument is that unbounded speculation may be let loose. Some controls or norms are, therefore, needed as criteria by which to judge. In our Jewish–Christian tradition we find these, as we shall later see, by reflection on the new creation, which for Christians becomes specifically the resurrection.

Each of these three fundamental issues highlights the tension between potential and limitation. Creation resounds with the potential of unlimited possibilities, but there are in fact limits to what there is and what is accessible to us. The priority of God emphasizes the potential of his freedom to do whatever he wishes, but contrasts it with the limitation implied by his stance of love. And the gap between what we finite human beings can imagine, our unbounded vision, and what we achieve, points in the same direction of potential and limitation.

Example: St Augustine

St Augustine provides a notable account of the personal disarray that may ensue when we grasp this tension of potential and limitation within ourselves and our world. He wished to have nothing to do with God, but found that God remained faithful to him and that flight was finally impossible, and confessed: 'You have made us for yourself and our heart is restless until it finds its rest in You' (*Confessions* 1.1). The remark is not distinctively Christian. It captures the general sense of dependent longing for security in the face of life's ambiguities. It might imply that Augustine wished to surrender his autonomy by giving up responsibility for his behaviour and settling for quietism. Some, both within the Christian community and outside, argue that this is precisely the nature of Christian faith and commend Augustine's frankness.

But there is another possibility. Augustine makes his dependence conscious and is thus able to resume his responsibilities as a human being. He is describing the basic human dilemma between surrendering and acknowledging responsibility.

FAITH DESPITE MYSELF

The more we become aware that we are autonomous beings, the more we simultaneously discover the frustrations which are imposed from inside and outside ourselves. So the more sensitive and alert we are to our autonomy, and the more eager we become to act on the responsibilities that go with it, the more we realize that the only way to its exercise is by surrendering parts of it. To develop potential we have to come to terms with limitations. Caught in this lived dilemma, we are bound from time to time to regress to our primary condition of dependence. We may view such regression either as a weakness or as a description of a process which is a necessary part of ourselves and our worlds. This movement between the world as it is, our dependent life within it, and our contribution to it, is the foundation of the Christian understanding of the creation.

CREATION AND DEPENDENCE IN HUMAN EXPERIENCE

Dependence and creation go hand in hand. Our lives begin merged with our mother and relying upon her (or, after birth, some other). Psychological 'birth' does not take place at the same time as physical birth, but begins as we go through the processes of becoming individuals. However, the sense of reliance on another persists, and throughout our adult life, however mature we may become, at various moments we revert to it. Dependence, therefore, is not opposed to individuality or autonomy. All three are complementary aspects of those processes which create and sustain us as people and which manifest themselves both in individual and in group behaviour. They are integral to our being as creatures. But creatures are not complete in themselves, unchanging or immortal. Creatureliness is perennially reasserted through three experiences which are common to us all: death and decay; the sense of history, or time passing; and our awareness that experience itself is fragmented. But as a way into exploration of God, our creaturely dependence looks promising.

Decay and death

Both personal ageing and cosmic entropy mark mortality. Death is not only the final boundary to our known existence as embodied beings; it is also the key paradigm of many other boundaries over which we make transitions as we move through life. Every shift that we make in our growth involves losing the security of the state which is being left. The earliest distinction we draw is between 'I' and 'Not-I'. But to take advantage of this we first have to lose our previous perception of an undifferentiated world and the security such a notion offers. We repeatedly undergo these endings until we die. And the inevitability of this ultimate experience, death, which cannot be experienced, is so influential that people may sometimes be so inhibited by it that they are unable to face some of these lesser endings or transitions and become neurotic.

The impulse to religious belief might be regarded as a response to this inevitable sense of loss. Faced with the reality of our mortality, the argument runs, we cast around for security A reductionist sequence follows: religious conviction is a function of basic narcissism, concern with the self; this in turn is a response to the fear of death; reacting against this we create our gods as an infantile fantasy to enable us to cope with unfaceable reality, and this dependent stance accentuates our childlike helplessness by submission to a real or imagined leader or authority figure – God.

This 'explanation' of religion is trite and superficial. Religious belief is not necessarily a psychologically defensive stance; it could be, and in practice may prove to be, a constructive aspect of human functioning and not compensatory. But even if we dismiss the argument, the content remains important. Religion is indeed from some perspectives a response to human anxiety about the ending, our mortality and ultimate death, which are integral to our being created. Death strikes at the roots of our being and must make us anxious, whether we are conscious of this or not. Religious experience, therefore, is inevitably tied up with profound psychological roots. They are embedded in our unavoidable dependence, both physical and psychological, which follows from our being created. As a result, an authentic religious experience cannot achieve meaningful integrity without reviving the psychological roots that establish the possibility of trust on a higher level of spiritual maturity.

Sense of history

In common human experience reflection on history is not a sophisticated activity. It occurs all the time as individuals or groups create or demonstrate so-called 'facts'. Events are not so much obliterated or created (although both can happen) as reordered. We long for the security that a reliable past is believed to offer. We handle our anxieties about the present and future by reflecting on the past and unconsciously reordering it.

Our here-and-now experience thus becomes a mixture of past, present and believed future. But when it dawns on us just how fragile and ambiguous this mix is, we urgently seek certainty. In the flux of everyday human experience what has been gives us a notional fixed point. But using the past in our present and as an indicator, perhaps, of the future, we distort it; in a sense, therefore, we can be said to create it.

This reordering of history is another instance of dependence. A subtle process occurs as we revalue material which is already – at least in theory – publicly available. For example, children who are displaced from their families may create powerful myths about their origins. When these stories are examined they often illuminate crucial facets of that mélange of past, present and fantasized future experience that makes them individuals. Groups, nations and families do the same. Roots become important, and myths are woven around these to sustain assurance in the present. Religious institutions and claims to religious experience are a specific form of such behaviour. Past, present and future are fused, but the past tends to be held as normative, not least when there is stress in the present.

Fragmented experience

In Christianity instances of this dependent reordering of history regularly reappear as fundamentalism: biblical (back to the text), ecclesiastical (back to the tradition), or charismatic (back to the original – note, not just any – experience). Each is used to authenticate religious life by reference to a believed security which is derived from history. The third mark of mortality is the way in which the variety and different intensity of experiences fragment our sense of life as a whole. Experience is often spoken of as if it were an undifferentiated entity, although we distil particular experiences and give them different value. But the more we draw such distinctions the more unconnected our experiences become. We begin to wonder whether any coherence is possible.

One option, then, is to seek something outside us to contain the confusion for us. For example, the idea of God can be used to hold together incoherent experiences and thus imply that there is hope of integration. But this can only be when he himself is fully known, either in this world or the next. Coherence is an attribute of God and we trust it as the point around which to orientate the broken bits of our experience.

An alternative approach may be to develop an internal ordering system. Some people use therapy as a means to self-understanding and so give these procedures their status as quasi-religions. Others assert that all experience is relative and that incoherence is intrinsic to life. They make relativism their ordering model. We may argue about which is the best or correct way to deal with this issue, but whatever method is adopted, the aim is the same – to ward off personal disintegration.

This sense of fragmentation is integral to common human experience. The more we reflect on what happens to us, what we do and what we feel, the more awesome becomes the way in which social systems and people relate to each other. The problem of integration is bound to be addressed through dependence, although it may be heavily disguised. For example, the pluralistic society puts a premium on individual autonomy, which emphasizes personal sincerity and integrity. But in order to achieve this it underplays the obvious fact that autonomy is not a personal attribute and that each individual is autonomous only in relationship and relatedness to others. So personal autonomy itself can become as fantasized a dependable object as any other – a 'god'.

The experience of such fragmentation raises the spectre of being abandoned. Without a coherent context within which to set the welter of confusions that make up our common human experience, we feel alone. That is bad enough. But then the world sometimes begins to feel hostile too. It is not that it is over against us, but in our isolation we become introspective. We discover anew our lack of internal structure to cope with the disorientating nature of our world. This leads to an irrational fear that the world will somehow retaliate against us for our failure – unless we have some protection, we are bound to suffer retribution. These anxieties, which lie deep within us, give rise to a dependent response, which we express in dependent behaviour towards some other. This may be God or a structuring of relationships between people and things. But the aim and the effect is to make the world believably reliable and thus habitable.

THE MARKS OF DEPENDENCE

Three marks of dependence are notable in daily life. First, there is our wish that some dependable object should be available. In religion, for instance, it is not enough for God to be reliable; he must also be accessible to his worshippers. Second, there is a corresponding tendency to deny that we are responsible for ourselves and our actions. We try to load this on to others and to avoid taking and using our authority. We flee accountability as human beings for our various roles (parent, child, teacher, leader, etc.) and our individual or corporate responsibility. Third, as an outcome of this interaction, we begin to believe that things can be achieved without our personal involvement and at no cost to us; somehow others will do what is necessary and we can reap the benefit. This underlies our perennial longing for magical solutions to life's complexities. The magician knows how and what to do; the audience has only to watch or participate on his terms. He produces wonders without making demands, except on our credulity, which we willingly sacrifice.

While Christianity has frequently been contrasted with magic, we should recognize the propensity towards it which is encouraged by a further significant dimension to our estimation of creation: it includes God's loving disposition towards his creatures. Within the dependent dynamic the notion of love can be transformed into that of a comfortable haven into which we may securely settle. God's assumed reliability then becomes benignly welcoming and it can seem a sign of spiritual maturity for us to hand over to him our personal responsibility. Response to God's love subtly turns into doing something for his benefit: we unconsciously behave as though he needs us to depend on him, so that he is reinforced as God and the world becomes safer.

This religious fantasy – rarely articulated – underlies some individual piety and, in its social form, folk religion. It is the dynamic basis of apotropaic, or averting, magic, which surfaces from time to time in the idea, for example, of a votive offering. It sustains the idea of a beneficent God without any need to struggle to discover what it means to be human in this world.

HUMAN AND DEPENDENT

Four aspects of human behaviour focus in God as creator: our need for assurance about the ultimate boundary of known life; our sense of past, present and future; our longing to find coherence for our fragmented experience; and our willing collusion with any magic which might seem to release us from responsibility. Such behaviour is easily labelled 'dependent'. But dependence is more subtle and pervasive in human life and experience even than these aspects. We are facing the primary factor of human psychology, which is given and inescapable within the created order. It permeates our behaviour as finite creatures, often sustaining fantasies that make a sense of powerlessness or childishness legitimate.

But this is not a whim; dependence also represents a crucial developmental stage, which is incorporated into our continuing growth and remains part of what we are as human beings. And the fantasies which provide security and a means of coping with anxiety are fundamental attributes of our creatureliness, and not insignificant personal or social myths. Unless pastors as theologians can relate this whole area of life to God, we are excluding a huge dimension of human experience from theological consideration. Theologians and worshippers alike speak about the ways in which God and his creation 'relate' to each other. But behind that word lies a complex of ideas which needs to be clarified. Therefore, before addressing the specific question of God and dependence, we need a short excursus to clarify three terms, all rooted on 'relate'.

RELATIONSHIP, RELATEDNESS AND INTERRELATION

'Relationship' describes links between persons. It implies self-giving, as one person takes an initiative or responds to another. It is widely employed both in theology and in pastoral ministry. It characterizes a view of God which gives prominence to divine grace – God's self-giving and self-disclosure. Relationship stresses mutuality, since in any relationship both parties must be capable of responding to each other.

By contrast, 'relatedness' describes how people relate to each other through their different roles and how they connect with concepts, ideas and stances. So, for example, when we think of the human race as a sub-system within the larger system of creation, the connection between God and human beings is appropriately described in terms of their relatedness. This does not mean that the creature somehow has two parts, one capable of relationship and the other only of relatedness. The language simply makes clearer the type of relating that predominates at any moment.

Third, there is 'interrelation'. This ungainly word acknowledges that connections between people, whether as persons or in role, whether relationship or relatedness, are always reciprocal. A series of complicated dynamics can be discerned between persons or between an individual and a group. Within the individual, too, dialogue takes place between his person and his role. The word 'interrelation' reminds us of the obvious, but easily overlooked, point that, in addition to whatever the relationship and relatedness between two people or groups may be, the fact of their relating itself has an effect. It creates a new context which affects those involved and others.

Example: father and daughter

Between the father and his daughter there is a relationship. For the father it probably begins before her birth. But for both from her birth there is a maturing person-to-person contact in which each is affirmed by the other through reciprocal love. Looking from another perspective, however, we can discern a relatedness between them in a social context. They occupy roles, father and daughter, to which in society certain and different responsibilities attach. It is confusion by one or both of them of their relationship with their relatedness that produces inappropriate behaviour. The father loses sight of the daughter and sees only a woman. The daughter may collude. So their interrelation creates an incestuous context, which encourages secrecy. This may be found in the family, too, which turns this into a family secret. This affects them and others, chiefly members of the family, but also a wider range of people with whom they are in touch.

GOD AND DEPENDENCE

We may now return to the question of God and dependence. The longing that someone should be dependable is expressed in the demand that they should be immediately available. We desire the dependable object, whoever or whatever that may be, to be unfailingly on hand to do what is needed. We may contrast this dependent attitude with independence and dismiss it as immature. But when we assume that independence is the mark of personal maturity, we oversimplify matters by excluding a third possibility: mature life is marked by the confident exercise of autonomy based upon satisfactory management of dependence.

Immature dependence – the longing to be relieved of responsibility for our lives and the wish for magical solutions – locks us into questions of relationship alone. We become preoccupied with how dependable our partner – whether God or a fellow human being – is and less concerned with what we might achieve together. Mature behaviour in the context of such dependence, however, puts greater reliance on relatedness: we still value people for who they are but emphasize our mutual responsibilities, which derive from our distinctive roles.

When relationship and relatedness are both employed, a person may then become sufficiently confident to explore the complex interrelations between her, the world and others. But two conditions must be fulfilled if such a quality of living is to be achieved: first, we need the security of being aware of our role; and second, we also need that personal assurance which comes from being able to acknowledge and live with our dependence.

Examples will make the importance of these distinctions clearer and indicate their significance for theological thinking. One is drawn from human development and the other from the biblical tradition.

Example: the growing child

First, take a child. As she grows she shifts with increasing confidence and competence between being dependent and autonomous. Sometimes she is more dependent, sometimes more autonomous. But her growth in maturity is disclosed as she progressively understands that she really lives in interdependence with her mother and others. Realizing this, a good mother knows that the child needs to be encouraged to move away from and back to her. This shows in public behaviour in the park or on the beach. The child runs to and from mother. But this represents an internal process of oscillation as she progressively orders her world by risky development (going a little further each time) and comforting regression (coming back and finding mother reliably there). Mother may sometimes draw a limit: the child is going too far too soon. But if she is to become an adult she needs increasingly to claim her autonomy. In order to achieve this desirable aim she also has to be able from time to time securely to regress to her original felt dependence, both for reassurance but also to enable her to reflect upon the restructuring of herself which is what we call growth. She does not leave dependence behind; she uses it differently.

A mother's job is to manage the conditions so that her child can both move to independence and regress to dependence. Such managed regression is crucial; without it exploration of autonomy produces anxiety, making us less confident in facing the next demand, whether as child or adult.

Example: Moses and the burning bush

When Moses comes upon the burning bush (Exodus 3.1–12), each phase is clear: first, he is not surprisingly unsure in the presence of God or his emissary (3.6); second, God gives some command or announces a decision (3.10); third, God and Moses then negotiate what they intend jointly to achieve (3.11–12). Falling in awe, the human partner attributes all power to God and little or none to himself. He impotently adopts a posture from which he can contribute little or nothing. The second phase shifts him away from this personal relationship towards a sense of relatedness. By giving a command God affirms him in his role as creature and confirms his authority as such. On that basis man and God are each established in roles which enable usable contact to take place. Once that is affirmed, negotiation, or interrelationship, begins and achievement ensues.

We see here, as with human development, the shift from dependence to creative interdependence and the importance of managed regression. In these stories it is managed as God first accepts his human creature's fear and awe and transforms it by shifting the ground of the encounter through the personal affirmation of relationship to the more task-orientated dimension of relatedness.

Each of these illustrations, drawn from very different sources, shows that the primitive side of our human dependence cannot be disregarded or discounted. If God engages with us at the level of mature dependence alone, requiring articulated response and rational behaviour, this will not do. This assumption usually lies behind the general use of the word 'relate' in both theological and pastoral contexts. But it limits theologians and leads to some of the frustrations that many ministers, especially those who are theologically acute, experience in their pastoral work.

For example, in the doctrine of creation, reliability is an essential ingredient. Creation's order is the outworking of coherence in God himself. This sense of relatedness to our context is the foundation on which we have built both our scientific view of the world and our theological explorations. Reliability, order and relatedness, with their attention to interrelation, address aspects of mature dependence and how it may be harnessed for creativity. But God's engagement with his creation cannot be confined to this one facet of dependence. What of the immature dependence which is another mark of our human experience and behaviour? It cannot be ignored on the grounds of irrelevance or a belief that people do or should grow out of it. The psychodynamically informed view of human life shows that we do not grow out of it. Indeed it is frequently manifested in religion.

One way, therefore, to approach this complex but deeply felt issue could be through this question: What is the significance of the phenomenon of religion for the doctrine of creation?

DEPENDENCE, RELIGION AND CREATION

Pastors know that working with dependence is like swimming in a lake of glue. Religious leaders and simple believers meet this in their dealings with popular or folk religion: no sooner do you think that you have extricated yourself than you are trapped again. This is basic assumption dependence in a pure form: the wish for magic; the irrational hope that results may be achieved without personal commitment; profound anger when they are not; and a persistent expectation, which sometimes amounts to demand, that God should be immediately effective.

Pastors are generally suspicious of this sort of religion and on the whole theologians do not take it seriously into account. Those who have difficulty in living with the reality of this immature dependence, whether in themselves or others, may sometimes in the interests of faith seek to discount religious experience as data.

But no one engaged in pastoral ministry can go along with such polarizing. That is to ignore, or even discard, a major area of human behaviour with which we live. Pastors have to take a theologically more positive view of religion and claims to religious experience. When Feuerbach and Freud criticized religion as a particular instance of projective behaviour they were offering a reasonably accurate interpretation of some dimensions of religion. This scarcely needs to be discussed when we look at the evidence around us and in ourselves. But their further restriction of the discussion of what that evidence may signify must, however, be challenged. We need not worry about the answer to the question: Is God a projection of human need for a father figure? The crucial issue for the theologian and pastor is functional and arises within the stance of experimental faith: What is the significance of the projections and fantasies about a divine father figure for our concept of God?

The first question implies that religious believers construct a fantasy world which suits their dependent needs and so relieves their anxieties. There is little point in responding to such a view with ideas of reasonable religion and rational faith. What lies behind the question is not amenable to articulate argument. It raises the issue of ineradicable dependence, from which there is no escape – nor should there be a desire for escape. In firm believer, half-believer and sceptic alike there is a persistent feeling of suspicion that there is something in the suggestion because it addresses something primary in us as a result of our being created. Reason alone, therefore, cannot speak to this question. The pastor as theologian presses a different issue: given this dependence, immature and mature, what creative use of it might God make? Because this dynamic runs powerfully through our individual and corporate life, God, if he is to be the ultimate referent for religious experience, may be expected somehow to acknowledge this behaviour and reveal how he is prepared to meet us in it.

Worship, that characteristically religious (though not specifically Christian) activity, comes to mind. In worship people claim to encounter God. Worshippers place themselves consciously in the context of God and offer adoration. But in so doing they do not function solely at the rational level of mature dependence. Worship is also a way of making immature dependence sufficiently conscious for us to harness it to our way of living. The postures adopted, for instance, demonstrate this. And the claim that we offer all of life in worship may be more true than we had hitherto realized.

People take part in order to reaffirm, and have reaffirmed, their autonomy as God's creatures and so resume a life of deliberate interrelation with God and their contexts. The traditional Christian description of this is 'our neighbour'; and as a result of worship, life with him, her or them may become marked by confident interdependence. We need to match this practical interpretation to the theological question of why God might expect the worship of his creation. Part of the answer to that is that we are like this by virtue of our creation and our inevitable dependence. We contribute to creating a supernatural figure, and in worshipping it (her or him) address aspects of ourselves.

But we cannot end the matter there. As we have begun to see, while dependent behaviour is a significant ingredient of what it means to be human, dependence is a complex aspect of ourselves. We may identify the immature dependence which is seen in the longing for a 'god' and worship of him. But because of the multifaceted dimensions of human dependence, it is a mistake in a religious context to consider only one type of this – immature dependence. We cannot deal with the evidence for this without examining the significance of mature dependence.

The theological question has also to be taken further. It has generally been shaped in terms of God and creation. But the way this is done in fact restricts the range of examination. That is why few, if any, religions stop there. Belief in God and an ordered creation are fundamental, but religious people discover that their experience continually pulls them beyond the stage of merely affirming order. Religious language reflects experience. It is not full of indicatives alone. It is the language of the subjunctive (what might be) and the optative (what we wish could be). Therefore we find in our Jewish–Christian tradition that no doctrine of creation is complete without some corresponding idea of new creation.

In the Christian scheme this becomes the classic of the resurrection. We must turn to this before we can bring together dependence as a whole, both immature and mature. For if with this doctrine we enter the world of fantasy and imagination, which is one dimension of our dependent stance as creatures, we can do so only within particular parameters. Or, to put it another way, although the idea of God as Creator seems to be common to religion, it is not affirmed apart from some specific belief which gives it content that can be experienced. In Judaism, for example, this content may be the continuing survival of the people of God. In Christianity, however, it is the doctrine of the new creation or resurrection.

CHAPTER SIX

On the third day he rose again: the doctrine of the resurrection

The resurrection remains where it always was – central and controversial. It draws together four main strands of the Christian faith. Although the notion of a special event seems to contradict the coherence implied by the one unique divine act of creation, the resurrection is held to be a similar act of special divine initiative and creativity. Second, the resurrection cannot be construed apart from the life and death of Jesus Christ. When, as happens from time to time, the resurrection is divorced from the crucifixion, it then in effect annuls rather than confirms the way of the cross. Third, this doctrine always includes a future reference: the resurrection does not mark the end of the Jesus saga but is the point at which the end of all things begins. And fourth, people have persistently found, however often the logic of the argument is questioned, that Jesus' resurrection in some way witnesses to personal survival after death.

These four points remain in contemporary debate. Yet the idea of the resurrection itself challenges the coherence of the world on which we construct our lives, including our scientific thought. It feels easier and appears more reasonable to change our belief than to restructure the whole world and our ways of thinking. Another issue concerns knowledge of God. If God's revealed self lies beyond our usual definitions of rationality, then the common ground on which religious experience and theological thinking are founded crumbles. What sort of interchange can occur between people and God, if each inhabits such a different world of reason that communication is impossible? Religious and reasonable people alike find that they cannot live within the Christian tradition.

The question of a unique event is no problem. There is nothing intrinsically odd about such an idea; every event is unique. But in a religious context, where believers claim the uniqueness of the resurrection, such a tenet becomes impossible. It seems to destroy any sense that God might be accessible to us and that we might be able to discourse with him.

THE RANGE OF ISSUES

Around these points debate and argument still rage. But none of them can be isolated from the experience of the religious person. They concern our knowledge of ourselves and of our world; whether God can be known; and, even if he can, whether there can be any interchange with him.

Much work has been done on the philosophical, historical and textual questions concerning the resurrection. But since it also raises issues about the dynamics of human behaviour, we should see what illumination we might gain if we adopt a perspective based on that at the end of the twentieth century. Aesthetic thought on imagination and beauty is once more being increasingly acknowledged in the notion of 'elegance'. We leap back behind the massive edifice of nineteenth-century thought to recover the idea of order in relation to form.

AESTHETIC SCIENCE

For example, exploration of our universe goes in two congruent directions: outwards to the vastness of space and inwards into the microcosmic particles of matter. Hypotheses, especially those that seek unifying theories for both explorations, are elaborated in terms of elegance and beauty. What we know of the way our brains work seems to complement this emphasis. In the interaction between the hemispheres, one is chiefly concerned with logical thought and the other with imaginative creativity. Symmetry is required for intellectual and artistic creation. Together these can stimulate thinking on the resurrection. We might consider it in terms of the symmetry that it represents within the divine scheme of things. God's achievement lies in the way that he confirms the elegance of his creation by aligning imaginative creativity – a new creation – with the logical order of the coherent universe – creation itself.

Beauty and elegance can be contemplated and even adored. But they also have a function, which is best described as heuristic – enabling people to learn by their distinctive hands-on process. The use of elegance in the face of intractable problems presented by logical thought can circumvent the block. Instead of building an argument step by logical step from the base upwards, we make connections which seem and feel right, but which we cannot wholly justify, and so construct the superstructure and test how we may then build down to the foundation. In Jewish–Christian thought this connection between elegance, beauty and creativity permeates wisdom, a tradition that can also inform practical pastoral behaviour.

THE OPENNESS OF FIELDS

A further topic concerns the way that knowledge and understanding connect at different, but compatible, levels. This is the theory of the openness of fields, according to which it is axiomatic that in any complex organization each separate system must be open both upwards and downwards. It is open downwards in the sense that it must co-ordinate with certain basic statements; no system can start its own life out of the blue. But it is also open upwards in the sense that it cannot contain all its consequences; it is a means of serving a greater end. This implies that no formalized system of thought can be both consistent and complete at the same time.

The creation is one such complex organization, interpreted through a whole range of different schemes of understanding. One of these consists of theological affirmations, based upon people's belief; another may be composed of historical statements. The link between theological affirmations and historical statements is not optional; however different in status, they must connect. The resurrection offers a particular instance of how this theory applies. Without both personal affirmation and history – the order in which they come does not matter – there is no doctrine of the resurrection. By trying to think about the resurrection in the context of this theory of open fields, we discover that it is not a matter of private religious discourse but concerns human knowledge in general. It has to be articulated in terms which are compatible with interpretations of common human experience.

We also have to think of it in the setting of the larger field of creation. As a result, if we wish to claim that what we profess is complete, then it must be inconsistent. Alternatively, if we wish to stress its consistency, then we shall have to acknowledge that what we say is going to be incomplete. Our inevitable dependence, especially for that certainty which we immaturely expect, urges us not to recognize these obvious points. It demands both consistency and completion, and presses any who profess a belief in the resurrection magically to resolve the dilemma.

STORY AND NARRATIVE

We may also note the renewed prominence that is being given to story and narrative in the development of faith. We use stories to make connections between our past and the present. Their evocative power stimulates responses and the involving side of story conveys information. Thus they transform us when we make these stories our own. There is nothing remarkable about this. The procedure of constructing and using stories lies, for example, at the heart of dynamic therapy. The patient constructs a story, which is not history – the past – but is the past and present combined to create an interpretative story. The past is not recovered; it is used in the present to construct a way of interpreting life now.

Or to take another instance, a social worker may try to work with a fostered or adopted child by creating together a scrapbook of known bits of their life as a way of helping them locate themselves in the world. Again, this does not construct history; it generates enough of a story, which the child may use as a means of sorting himself or herself out.

THE NARRATIVE AS STORY

The resurrection narratives are stories in this sense. When we read and hear them, we can discern qualitatively different material from the pre-crucifixion stories of Jesus. The most significant difference lies in the way that the role of the hearer as one who contributes to the message being conveyed is made explicitly plain. The characters in the stories create the story itself. This is not about either Jesus or his disciples, but about the interaction between them. Neither alone creates the narrative; it stands as a product of their dealing with each other. If we extract one or the other, the story collapses. Therefore, there is no account of the resurrection itself – a point which the Gospel writers all emphasize. There are only stories about appearances, and an appearance is generated as much by those who see it as by those who are the object perceived.

The issues seem to become depressingly over-complex. However, from these technical questions, with which we are confronted, a fact which is of crucial importance to the pastor emerges: when dealing with this belief, we are not in the realm of rational human behaviour alone. Much effort has been expended in trying to make the doctrine amenable to our rational minds. Some argue that in the story of Jesus Christ we can hear the call to personal decision only when we recognize that the historical detail lies beyond recovery. That frees us to believe, to act and to research. Others present the resurrection as a historical event, open to scrutiny and providing evidence that demands faith. Yet others regard it as a powerful symbol within the framework of the history of religion. By contrast with this universal symbol of human hope, the resurrection has also been promoted as a description of intense personal experience.

Finally to these we may add the bolder approach which argues that within the prevailing view of history the resurrection is improbable, if not inconceivable. Christians, therefore, need to redefine what is meant by 'history', so that, by using the category of apocalyptic, the resurrection becomes the norm not the oddity. Apocalyptic is a dimension of wisdom literature that was undergoing something of a revival about the time of Jesus. For all its mystery and extravagant imagery, apocalyptic claims to show the world as it is. And in such a world a resurrection would not be so unlikely.

These difficulties are strongly felt, but the proffered solutions seem to take us away from the world of everyday human experience. They fail to deal with our felt longings about God (or some such transcendence), which become explicit in religious experience, essentially because they are too rational. We have already seen that dependence is a complex dynamic that includes within it aspects of ourselves which lie deeper than rationality.

RESURRECTION AND CURIOSITY

When we think of common human experience, and of religious experience in particular, we include the significance of its irrational aspect. This is not a weakness to be therapeutized away, but a facet of our selves that can be recognized and used. But if it is ignored, it may return in bizarre ways. This is certainly true of its religious manifestations. And in thinking about the resurrection we are in an area where the rational and irrational appear to coincide. These are complex issues which are illuminated by a specific appreciation of curiosity.

Creation's order stimulates our curiosity. It challenges us to struggle to extend the frontiers of our knowledge. Whatever the contemporary disillusionment with science, our era remains one of curiosity. Largely because of the easy availability of the media, this is no longer restricted to a few. And this curiosity is not confined to our interest in the world around us. It is a critical factor in the way that we develop as individuals and relate to one another in families and other social groups.

Families in which members display delinquent behaviour are also frequently marked by a lack of interpersonal curiosity. People seem to prefer not to know about each other or their relationships. As a result family members are often extraordinarily certain that they know, understand, and can speak for the experience of others in the family. Usually those involved collude in assuming that such understanding is possible in order to avoid the obvious point that it is impossible to understand other people's behaviour, and probably not even your own. We might risk interpretation, but that is another thing altogether from understanding.

Adam and Eve assume knowledge about each other's lives, their relationship with each other, and their relatedness in their roles as human creatures to God the creator. They do not need to explore because of this assumption. As a result their personal relationship is corrupted, their intimacy with God is shattered and the world of nature becomes destructive. Without curiosity we become less than human and less competent at taking up roles. The result is that communal and individual pathologies increase.

Why does pathological behaviour increase? Often it is a result of the parents' inability to tolerate ambiguity and uncertainty. If they can recover this, other members of the family may become able to reorientate their inner worlds and so develop a new style of relating to each other. They begin to admit that they do not in fact understand another person's feelings, but that through participation they can appreciate enough of their own to be useful to others. Gradually a new discovery is made: what happens between members of a family not only affects them; it affects other members and thus there reappears the genuine unit – the family.

This process throws valuable light on the idea of the resurrection. If we grasp that the essence of sin may be regarded as the absence of curiosity, then salvation occurs in so far as this capacity is restored to us. For that to happen to creatures the first response has to be from the creator, who proves himself willing to tolerate ambiguity and uncertainty about himself and can be believed to do so. Creation, with its emphasis on coherence and rationality, and its demand for mature dependence on the part of the creature in relation to the creator, is by itself inadequate to support such an idea. For it does not sufficiently address our immature dependence. This, however, is what we find being handled when we turn to the new creation or resurrection.

The resurrection stands within the Christian faith as the place where God acknowledges our immature dependence, and the irrational behaviour that is often connected with it, as a significant facet of the human being and one which he considers worth stimulating and investing in. The stories, as well as the idea itself, emphasize ambiguity and have always aroused correspondingly ambivalent responses in disciples, from the time of the New Testament to the present day. There is a naughtiness about the whole idea, as if what ought not to happen does, and a playfulness about the stories. The confines of order, or of pathological certainty, are broken by God's quizzical invitation to be curious. This is not the so-called detached curiosity of the scientific observer, but the intimate curiosity of human relations, which directs us to interrelationships. We cannot separately interpret ourselves or others; we can only interpret both and explore how they connect for the benefit of each.

This process exposes to us the significance of our irrational selves, an experience which is fraught with risk but is ultimately humanizing. The resurrection cannot be examined in terms of reason alone. Our rational selves seek understanding of our lives, the world – even of God. But there are also the parts of ourselves about which we can only risk interpretation. These draw us nearer the edge of existence, where our rational selves seem less all-embracing and significant, and our feelings, irrational when thought about but essential for our being ourselves, take over.

Yet even when allowance is made for the wide range of possible interpretations, this doctrine arouses particularly fierce passions and divisions. There are those who believe most firmly, and those who will not believe at all. The resurrection polarizes belief; believers and unbelievers alike respond. Few remain completely agnostic, although sometimes this excuse may be offered for vacillation. But these divisions are not solely between believers and non-believers. Within the believer (and maybe also in the unbeliever) there is a split between the dependent longing ('If only God would do something sure and dramatic') and the need to test reality which derives from faith in God the Creator ('God does not demonstrate his presence by miracles of this type'). Both feelings are aroused by the idea of resurrection, and complement each other.

The resurrection, therefore, is both professed by the committed believer and is a focal point for unbelief. But it is also the theological means by which we begin to value such unbelief, since the believer's questions are not peculiar to him or her. They are instances of basic human experience – dependent longing for the irrational sides of ourselves to be affirmed and the need for rational testing of reality – and the tension that these two facets generate. This is important for the pastor as she struggles to link her distinctively Christian faith to the folk beliefs of those among whom she ministers. The two are not separated by any test of belief in the resurrection.

This core tenet of the faith, however, can now be seen as the specific point of contact which God provides for that immature dependence which is the chief mark of folk religion. The resurrection is therefore not a private Christian subject; it deals with issues which lie at the core of common human experience. An essential foundation of human life – curiosity, which is of the essence of common human experience – again emerges at the heart of the Christian confession. One of the marks which defines that faith – the resurrection of Jesus Christ – turns out to be a focal affirmation both for religious experience and confession and for common human experience.

The interpretation of everyday life in the light of the gospel is the pastor's task. Here is a primary point of contact for such interpretation, provided that she can escape the restricting tyranny of rationality, whether in herself, her fellow Christians or in those with whom she is ministering. With her feelings, therefore (and consequentially her irrational parts), she can begin to make and use connections between her distinctively Christian profession, which motivates her, and the expectations and demands which people might make. If these connections fail, then, as with the absence of curiosity – or, as we might say, with sin – the unities of creation are destroyed, not least the way that men and women of every and any persuasion have life in common to explore. When the resurrection becomes the private concern of the believer, it also ceases to be a life-sustaining belief and becomes a point of internal controversy. And for the rest of the world a story, which exposes the importance to God of both the irrational parts of ourselves and our immature dependence, is made inaccessible.

CURIOSITY AND WORK

The resurrection is the way in which God creates the conditions for working on this needful curiosity. It introduces imbalance into whatever secure stance any of us may have adopted. By encouraging curiosity about God and ourselves, believers or unbelievers, the resurrection creates a disturbance which can produce change. It will not allow us to escape to the haven of rationality or of irrational behaviour alone. Here we meet the dynamic equivalent of the heuristic process of discovery. The tension between these complementary facets of our being is recognized in the resurrection, but not resolved. Curiosity in families is stimulated and made creative by encouraging participation. Similarly the resurrection does not allow detached observation; it is not accessible as event alone. Nor, however, can it be sustained as a notion which has its origins in the believer alone.

This is why it is impossible precisely to locate the issue of the resurrection. It is neither wholly outside the believer (a matter of investigation) nor wholly inside (a matter for belief), but both inside and outside and at the boundary of our experience. This is exactly, but not now surprisingly, given the topic, the description of that constant negotiation that we have seen to be the arena of the pastor's role and person. This aspect of faith represents the claim that God endorses that necessary curiosity which runs through our human nature. For the pastor, the debilitation which results from the denial of such pervasive curiosity – sin – is daily manifested in the lives of those with whom she deals. But the central tenet of her faith, the resurrection, does not stand apart from this core dilemma of human life. On the contrary, it affirms that this creation is not only sustained by order and kept explorable by reason but is also enlivened by curiosity and the imaginative use of ourselves.

Common human experience, therefore, points the pastor to her central belief; her central belief refers her back to the heart of common human experience. This is the frequently described daily experience of ministry. But it now becomes manifestly congruent with a core Christian belief – the resurrection. In our pastoring, then, we are not dealing with the dynamics of human behaviour alone. We are discovering in the process itself part of God's interpretation of our human life at its unconscious level.

RESURRECTION AND PLAY

In our thinking about creation we can become so preoccupied with creativity and its results that we overlook the important dimension of play. Play is not confined to children. We all play when we act without discernible conscious motive or concern for a specific end. Play is performed for its own sake and carries its own value, 'the resolution of a dialectic between work and rest'.[1] Some of our undisclosed selves becomes momentarily discernible as we unselfconsciously express what we are through relaxation rather than by purposeful application:

> Play is paradoxical behaviour. Exploring what is familiar, prac-
> tising what has already been mastered – friendly aggression,
> sex without coition, excitement about nothing, social behaviour
> not defined by specific common activity or by social structure,
> pretence not intended to deceive: this is play.[2]

The resurrection narratives about the risen Christ are shot through with enigma and play. The empty tomb poses a riddle which persists throughout the history of the Church: 'Where is Jesus?' This is not a simple question requiring a single answer, but one which puts a supplementary demand on the enquirer: 'Where do you expect him to be?' or 'Where would you like him to be?' It is also worth reminding ourselves that the bulk of the material in the Gospels is not about the resurrection, but is in the form of encounter stories between individuals, groups and the risen Christ.

These stories, far from being incontrovertible evidence of the risen Christ, are marked by the disciples' ignorance and blind-ness. They seem to have little intrinsic value as evidence of more than that. But when we realize that they are describing play, they take on new power. Mary meeting the gardener is caught up in the twists of disguises and charades. The walkers on the road to Emmaus take part in the old game of blind man's buff. The con-fused behaviour of the group of disciples is exactly that of people caught between work and rest – that is, at play. Angels and mes-sages, appearances and confusion signify that the resurrection narratives are set in the sphere of games and play.

The concept of play again carries us beyond the realm of rational, consciously purposeful behaviour. We naturally need to beware of idealizing it. Like any other human activity, it takes place in the context of life and is not itself all of living. Nevertheless, this dimension to our experience reminds us that it is as mistaken to limit enquiry into the resurrection to what 'actually' happened, as it is to try and interpret our play and games, whether as adults or children, with the same restricted question. Our questions must be framed so as to admit answers which can include the irrational as well as the rational aspects to God's activity. If either of these facets is absent, God's engagement with us as we are will inevitably be inadequate.

CREATION AND RESURRECTION

The doctrine of creation presents God as a reliable focus for our legitimately dependent expectations. We are the creatures who look to our creator. The new creation, with its ambiguities and tensions, demonstrates that we are not confined to that dependent mode but are made with it so that we may harness it to work with God. To bring this about, God meets our dependent expectation at our most primitive unconscious level, where magic is sought. What is more, he further invites us to see him as he expresses through play new sides to his inner being. The question: 'What sort of God is it that raises Jesus from the dead?' does not now have to be answered solely in terms of the coherence of the universe.

Creative partnership with God sounds wonderful but feels beyond many of us, not least the ordinary pastor and Christian. But sharing in play is not. God reveals himself in an activity which is an end in itself and without ulterior motives. This is the activity in which he invites us to be his partners and in so doing discloses that our destiny, too, is play. No longer can we consider this aspect of life a pastime; it is the purpose for which we are created. We are invited to exist, like God himself, between work and rest, where we may truly claim that we are most obviously what we are made to be. Work is necessary as an alliance with the creator God; rest is desirable, to sustain perspective. But between the two we play, bringing the seriousness of reality and the range of our imagination into a harmony that generates new life in us and for others. As the Indian poet Rabindranath Tagore puts it, 'on the seashore of endless worlds children play'. The Christian is just such a child.

A revitalized sense of the dynamics of play in the resurrection gives new depth to a major question of our existence. This, as phrased in the opening question of the Shorter Catechism of Westminster (1648), is: 'What is the chief end of man?' The answer remains, even if expounded in new terms: 'Man's chief end is to glorify God and to enjoy him for ever.' The resurrection invites our involvement, calling us like children to be caught up in this specific instance of God's play. A delicate touch is needed to turn dependence to useful work.

In a dependent group, for example, the leader cannot deny members' expectations. If he does, destructive anger, either as violence or apathy, results. Equally he cannot merely endorse the dependence, since that reinforces its stultifying effect. The skill is to find the means to indicate that it is a necessary but debilitating condition. One effective way of doing this is through humour: the oblique comment can be more effective than the direct description. It acknowledges the dependence and simultaneously skews perceptions and thus brings about change.

Just these qualities are found in the God of the resurrection. There is a quizzically humorous quality to the accounts, which also marks the concept of resurrection itself. Through this central tenet of faith, in which our necessary curiosity can be stimulated and exercised, God enables us to live with the questions of magic which our dependent longings produce. These are the 'What if . . . ?' questions of life, which show by their form their origins in dependence. But the resurrection, while encouraging the dependent question, refuses to allow us an escape to magical answers. It asks the further question: 'What if such a thing did and does happen?' In so doing it forces us to address our many dependencies, wherever they appear in aspects of our lives, not only in our religious beliefs.

THE INTERPRETATION OF DEPENDENCE

The fundamental dynamic of our humanity – dependence, both mature and immature – is obliquely, tantalizingly and humorously interpreted by God's action. Inviting ultimate trust, he affirms that he is beyond us, offers us a point of supportive and affectionate recourse, and demonstrates that his vitality is free of our contribution. Because we are invited to share in this playing, we are driven to examine our internal world of created objects, including the God upon whom we each project. We can discover that God is not an hallucination, but one about whom we have to take a position. But, finally, we can realistically appreciate that his fate is to be relegated to limbo by most people, including at times ourselves.

There is a further aspect to play which needs a brief note. We are all fascinated by toys. It may be a longed-for present; it may be (to the donor's dismay) the box and not its contents. But whatever the case it is something we play with and use imaginatively. Among the most significant 'toys' in our life is that piece of blanket or toy animal or something of the sort from which at one stage in our lives we could never bear to be separated. It could not be washed, therefore it smelled; it usually had its own peculiar name. My godson's was a bit of old towelling called 'Bampti'. It could not be left, because without it we could not travel; and heaven help any mother who lost it – the response was inconsolable grief. This object helps us make the transition from being dependent on mother's presence to being able to conceive her in the mind without her being physically present. The move is vital for our growing into adults who are able to relate to others. This is known as 'a transitional object'. It begins to function unexpectedly: it cannot be forced upon a child. But also it suddenly ceases to be necessary: one day it is essential to living; the next it is discarded.

One way of thinking about God is as such a transitional object. That is not the full story, of course, but it is an extent to which some people, indeed possibly most people, experience religion in their life. An unsophisticated awareness of the spiritual dimension to the world can come at any moment. It may be to do with some deep human experience, such as a death or a wedding or rejoicing or sadness which impinges on us as something greater than it appears to be in itself.

In order to work through this we need some way of dealing with 'God' and he becomes for a period a transitional object. He is picked up, used and then discarded. This is one of the hardest matters for pastors: why do people after receiving some ministry, not stick with the church? It is because the church represents God, who, like the child's teddy bear, is picked up when needed and then thrown aside. It would be impossible to obtain evidence of this in any detail, but it is the impression from surveys that, when asked, many have some such experience.

RESURRECTION AND FOLK RELIGION

This last point brings us to the theological significance of folk religion.[3] The demand for ritual expression of confused, dimly felt, but nonetheless real, feelings is one which every pastor knows. Some regard it as residual or debased religion and argue that it is best ignored. But apart from being pastorally unwise, that stance is theologically damaging to the gospel. Folk religion has a theological function. By presenting us with belief in a God whom they had consigned to limbo, those who express folk religion take us to the heart of the classics of creation and new creation. The expressions of folk religion consistently direct us to the dimension of God's nature that has emerged from our behaviourally informed reflection on the resurrection.

Because dependence is an integral part of creation, people in general, albeit for the most part unwittingly, need believers and churches to sustain the possibility of belief in the continuing liveliness of God. Because churches, ministers and believers are available, they allow others to recall, as needed, the God they have relegated to limbo. But this recovery is not casual. There is bewilderingly intense feeling, often of possession and control, when people find churches or believers inadequate or unsuitable for this task. It surfaces when, for example the closure of a church building is announced or when a minister (for whom the generic term becomes 'vicar') is believed to have refused to baptize a baby. People with no obvious connection with the Church or sacraments suddenly emerge full of indignation.

The converse, however, may be less obvious: religious believers need those who have left God in limbo but who also retain in their make-up as dependent creatures something that we can characterize as religious experience. Otherwise believers may, in their sophisticated believing, ignore the irrational dimension to religious belief in themselves as well as in those with whom they are dealing. Some of the problems that ministers face lie precisely here: they become closed to these aspects of their own life and belief, and so cannot be sufficiently open to them in others. What is for the minister a minor facet of belief, can be for others the whole scenario.

The resurrection is central to the Christian faith; it is not, however, confined to the belief of the Church. This distinctive confession addresses a side of human behaviour that is fundamental for all, believer and unbeliever alike. This implies that the problems which we associate intellectually and emotionally with the doctrine of the resurrection should be kept as problems and not solved or explained. If we try to do this, however noble the reason, we excuse ourselves from facing basic dependence and so deny people the opportunity of discovering both that God engages with it and how he does so for them.

Example: the empty tomb

The question of the empty tomb is the key instance. Some wish to turn God into the magician of the resurrection by having him perform a major miracle. The resurrection is always in danger of appearing to be a magical trick, as God does something incredible and unique. This might not be too serious, except that it also assumes that he does this apart from any involvement on our part. It is his act alone and we are merely those who believe in it or contemplate it. If we take this view, then we have uncritically used the empty tomb to sustain our dependent longings. The story is then stuck in that particular dynamic, and it cannot function in any useful way, either for ourselves or, more importantly, to inform the pastoral and evangelistic ministry of the Church.

Another way of looking at this question, however, is to see that arguments for and against the tomb being empty represent identical wishes to avoid the internal anxiety that the ambiguity of the evidence for the resurrection arouses. Each assured conclusion – that it was empty, that it was not, that we cannot know – is a slide into immature dependence upon an unambiguous God. Either he does miracles, or he does not, or he remains beyond examination. But whichever position is adopted, it feels reliable to its proponent and gives a sense of security. Yet one stance is in fact no more mature or sophisticated than any other, since none of them allows the classic of the resurrection to function to interpret us out of our innate tendency towards reassurance of some kind. The controversy, therefore, for all its apparent cunning and sophistication, may merely keep us, believer and unbeliever alike, in an immaturely dependent and uncreative state.

The story of the empty tomb is a means by which God encounters our dependence, whatever form it takes. This may be our longing for magic in God, which, as we have seen, is addressed by the stories but with which there is no collusion. It may be a desire to be assured about our fate after death: does the resurrection guarantee future life or does it assure us that we do not survive? The former has on the whole been the historic Christian belief, the latter becoming more prominent in recent years. The empty tomb confirms neither, but it does direct us, as a tomb, to the mortality which is a reality to be faced by all. What is more, this story speaks to our dependence in that playful, humorous, but finally interpretatively serious, fashion that we have discerned in the whole complex of the resurrection.

The crucial question about the story of the empty tomb, therefore, is how it is brought to bear on whatever activity, new discovery or exploration is required in our lives or for others at any moment. It is most faithfully dealt with when we set it in the context of how we experience in ourselves and, so far as we can be aware, in others, the way that God acknowledges our dependent needs and interprets them into change and new life.

When we claim that God meets us at the level of our unconscious life, we include in this that he takes seriously the dependence with which we are imbued. This is how the central tenet of the resurrection and the fringe beliefs represented by folk religion are held together. There is an interaction which too sophisticated a solution or belief destroys. If believers lose the innocence of the folk-religious aspects of themselves by rejecting them in others, they will also find that they have lost the transforming power of the new creation. In the resurrection of Jesus God copes with the dependent feelings of his creation in such a way as to encourage work with him to continue. Our longing for magic is focused and expressed, but is not allowed to dominate. The resurrection meets our desire for magic without becoming magical. We cannot discard the sense of wonder, but equally this proves inadequate as the sole basis of our life in God's creation.

CONCLUSION

We should not isolate the resurrection within the nexus of foundational Christian doctrines: crucifixion and resurrection, creation and incarnation. It is the most broadening of them all, because in creation and resurrection (new creation) God handles that pervasive dependence which undergirds our existence. Incarnation (as we shall see) and crucifixion are primarily concerned with God's work and his invitation to us to co-operate with him. But creation and resurrection concern other dimensions, which have no discernible end or result. Crucifixion demonstrates the way in which that demand is to be lived and orders our spiritual life. But by contrast creation and new creation (resurrection) endorse activities which lack obvious purpose – self-giving in play, celebration and joy. Here is the necessity of belief in the resurrection.

CHAPTER SEVEN

Making all things new: creation, resurrection and pastoral care

Working ministers who have reflected on their daily experience as we have considered this double doctrine will have noticed that the discussion has moved between two extremes in the connection which is made between Christian faith and common human experience. On the one hand, the common experience is one of all-pervasive dependence – mature or immature, individual or corporate. The Christian faith, on the other hand, is specific in its affirmation of Jesus' resurrection. Although this belief includes ideas which can be found in religion in general, Christianity gives them distinctive definition in the resurrection.

People frequently express their feelings in generalized forms of religious behaviour. They turn up, for instance, for rites – baptisms, weddings and funerals. The minister may also be often asked for quasi-magical blessings. Pastors offer themselves and the Church as focal points where the specifically Christian gospel of Christ may be found, explored and, they hope, believed. Yet in a way that seems beyond their control they also indiscriminately figure in people's half-formed world of belief. The label 'Christian' covers a range of behaviour. Much is socially acceptable – being a good neighbour and behaving well. Allied to this is a general belief in some sort of God, who benevolently oversees the universe. Jesus Christ is worth respect, although definite claims about him are left to those who are publicly religious.

MINISTRY AND FOLK RELIGION

But ministers who believe that they should work with those who are not already integrated into the Church soon discover that they cannot draw a simple distinction between 'false' and 'true' belief. Folk religion employs Christian forms and language. If ministers, therefore, appear indifferent or even hostile, they may confusingly suggest that they are rejecting the belief that they themselves profess, or, at least, that they regard it as inadequate. This is probably why Christians spend time redefining, usually to little avail, other people's use of 'their' language.

But we may go further. If Christians are honest about their faith, they cannot dispense with folk religion. On closer inspection they find its characteristics inside themselves as well as others. The notion of folk religion can become simply a projection of the parts of Christian belief and practice which believers find unmanageable. They disown them, project them into vulnerable others and deal with them there. But this is exactly the stance which the gospel condemns.

Dependence is focused on the claim which is most distinctively Christian – the resurrection. So the more Christians fail to come to terms with the dependent longing for magic, the more it will return to haunt them in their profoundest beliefs. At the heart of professed Christian faith reside aspects of the marginal types of religious behaviour which constitute the pastor's usual working material. This may explain why folk religion is such a test for the pastor and why Christians become so disturbed when the resurrection seems to be questioned. The minister is not only being confused about who he is and how he is being used (the religious figure); he is also given a sense that as he deals with these 'peripheral' matters (as they seem) he may be undermining the core of his faith.

PASTORING, RITUAL AND PLAYFULNESS

One thing for which people legitimately look to the Church is ritual. A church that does not worship is a contradiction in terms, and one that does not handle people's feelings and expectations through ritual is no longer distinctively a church. This is as true of requests for formal liturgical acts as it is of the approach of an individual to a minister for help. Someone asking a priest or minister for counsel does not necessarily consciously come to a religious figure. They are likely to be confused, otherwise they would not be there in the first place.

Ritual

The pastor is wise to ask himself why a minister of religion has been approached. Counselling services, usually confidential and often anonymous and free, are widely available. It may, of course, be that he is the last resort. But he should at least be sufficiently alert to what he may signify to be able to recognize that when many people come to a pastor, they do so in the unconscious expectation of some kind of religious response. Jesus' saying that a loving father, when a child asks for a fish, does not give him a snake, provides the paradigm for this activity (Luke 11.11). When pastors are, in however faint a fashion, implicitly invited to confirm guilt or sin and offer forgiveness or absolution, they fail if they provide only counsel or sympathy. There is a difference worth preserving between the penitent and the client, not least since this distinction often lurks in those who deliberately turn to the pastor.

Ritual plays an important part when forgiveness and absolution are sought. It is more important than today's somewhat limited stress on a liturgy derived from within the confines of early Christian history sometimes suggests. Like the resurrection, ritual displays the playfulness of God and its connections with the absurd and his humour. We take up special roles in order to help people make a transition from one state to another: guilty to forgiven, single to married, accompanied to bereaved, and so on. Sometimes such roles are emphasized by dress, language or style. Ministers in most traditions put on distinctive dress for ritual. For instance, a priest may put on a stole to hear a confession and pronounce absolution. The stole does not make any difference to the procedure, but it helps to establish basic conditions, such as presumed confidentiality and a formal acknowledgement that God stands behind all that is happening.

This is playful, in the sense that the dressing-up is not itself purposeful. It is one means of establishing the conditions in which work may be done. Those who on grounds of theological principle reject this may be missing a critical point in their dealings with people. Such playfulness does not trivialize. It has a very serious side, which emerges in two long-standing pictures of the pastor, as fool and as wise man, both of whom, incidentally, are usually identified by their appearance – the fool's cap and the wise person's wizened visage or beard.

The fool is given licence to say what cannot be said. He occupies a privileged position – one in which ministers find themselves more frequently than they may realize. Discounted as other-worldly, or somehow preserved in people's belief as immune from sullying reality, they can become the fools of this world. Their fundamental foolishness is to believe at all. But they are also envied their foolery, since it gives them permission to handle parts of life which people know are there but which they find difficult to address. When the minister knows this he can say the unspeakable without being sententious. In the full sense of the word, he 'plays' with people in a constructive play like that of God in the resurrection.

Wisdom

The second aspect of this playfulness is wisdom. The long trad-ition of wisdom begins from a firm, but critical, belief in the intrinsic value of human life and its trivia. Like the pastor with the resurrection, it switches between the peripheral life of mankind and the heart of God himself. Absurd and humorous images often make vital points about individual and social life. Jesus places himself in this line as a wise teacher when he uses parables. It is the tradition of the ridiculous story but serious issue, and of the almost cynical, worldly wise minister, who with caustic love holds a perspective for others. Lightness of touch is matched to the seriousness of the topic.

In both instances – foolishness and wisdom – playfulness is a model for pastoral practice which expresses confidence in life's trivia. The motif of resurrection undergirds the pastor's ministry in this area. He can offer interpretation to people in their con-fusions, hopes and fears and their longing for some sort of magic. But he does not have to deny or abandon his own religious moti-vation and perspective to do this. He invites people to join him in a playfulness with their lives, recognizing how responsible they are in themselves and their various roles, their relationships, relatednesses and interrelations – but not ignoring their depend-ent selves, to whom God has responded in this central revelation of himself.

Minister not counsellor

Ritual behaviour – not just performing some ritual act, but thinking of ritual as a basis of ministry – reminds the pastor that she is a minister of God's playfulness, the gospel of resurrection. The counsellor seeks as a fellow human being to help distressed and disturbed people, and works from this perspective to create new ways of coping and living. That is a rough, but sufficient, description. The pastor, however, offers – and is used to provide – something different. She, too, is a fellow human being, but in addition she is also a representative of God and of a religious view of life. There will be a gap between the belief that motivates her and what she is expected to represent, but there is always this aspect to the encounter, as well as the interrelation of two individuals and their interaction. The counsellor tries to assist people restructure their lives by gaining a new perspective on themselves and their connections with others; this is the therapeutic process. The pastor works with the same material, people and their feelings, but with a view to educating the person to see life not just with a new perspective but in the specific context of God.

That is why in the New Testament pastoring is linked with teaching: the content of the Christian faith illuminates the practice of the pastor and is included in his resource for others, even those who do not believe. But for believers and others alike the educating work of pastoral practice releases energy which can bring about major change. In Christian language this means conversion in some sense. This may be fully to Christ and the Christian Church. But at its least it can be in the way that they view themselves, others and the world in the setting of the larger context that the idea of God represents.

Fool, but not an idiot

When the minister grasps this, two points follow. First, he need not be over-concerned about the apparent foolishness of the Christian gospel on which he bases his ministry. This is not only the foundation of his life and work; it is also what enables him to be involved with people at all. The playfulness of ritual is not just amusing; it is a latching-on point for ministry, since it is a way of affirming to ministers and those whom they meet that the context is God. The criterion by which to test any foolishness is whether it has become an end in itself. The fool may become the clown and then shift to being the idiot. That foolishness is not an asset but a liability. The test of the foolishness of God is whether it engages people's profoundest feelings, conscious and unconscious, whatever the outcome. The foolishness which is divine and which God expresses, at least in significant part, through his ministers is not a consciously self-generated stance, but derives from interaction with people's expectations. This, as we have seen, is exactly the character of the resurrection. It stands as a permanent challenge to the pastor of the creative foolishness of God as a practical notion.

RECOVERING CONFIDENCE

The second consequence is that the minister can recover confidence in making explicit use of the gospel. His interpretation of life needs to have Christian content, not by loading on to people stories or demands, which may seem unbelievable, but by embodying the faith that these have inspired. Thought of primarily in terms of function, the resurrection reminds ministers that presence and empathy alone, crucial as they are, do not satisfy people's expectations of the Church and its ministers – the hope of God. The freedom of wonder and imagination, and the large vision that can ensue, are endorsed by God in the resurrection. This constitutes the pastor's stance and the penitent's destiny.

Example: a story of ministry

This instance is drawn from everyday pastoral ministry and illustrates the significance of simple ritual activity, when performed with sensitivity and with some awareness of its significance.

A woman in the parish, who had nothing directly to do with his church, asked the vicar to call because her mother was dying. Some years previously her son had been in trouble and in prison on remand. At that time the vicar had heard and visited, spending a short time with her. This, however, was the extent of formal contact. They had occasionally met in the pub, but for three years prior to this episode he had not seen her at all and had assumed that she had left the district. She lived with her mother, the other sisters being some distance away. Her phone call to the vicar included the following passage: 'Please come, vicar. Mother is dying. The doctor has been and is looking after her, but she is not settled (*sic*). Please come and settle her.'

The minister visited, was welcomed by the woman and then went in to see the dying mother. She was sedated and comfortable; there was no apparent distress. After a brief talk, the pastor performed three ritual acts: he held the dying woman's hand; he spoke reassuringly to her; and he blessed her in the name of God. The daughter thanked him and he left, promising to call in the evening. But he was prevented by another demand and that night the old lady died. Yet, although the vicar had failed to appear, there was no anger or animosity when finally he visited again. The one thing the daughter wanted him to know was that, after his visit, her mother had been much more 'settled' (*sic*). She told her sisters how splendid 'John' (*sic*) had been over the old lady's death; how helpful he 'always' (*sic*) was; and specifically how he had helped her personally.

The facts were that, although she presumed intimacy with the minister by using his first name, she had never been near the church, and her sole serious contact with him had been for about one and a half hours some four years prior to her mother's death.

The minister might have thought that proper ministry required him to try and address the woman's fantasies about him and the Church, for example, by asking why she had called for him, what she really expected of him, how she saw her standing with God, or any similar questions. But whatever she, and more especially the dying woman, may have needed would probably have been overlooked. The mother had been professionally and expertly treated by her doctor, but she still wanted something that she could describe only as 'being settled'. Such settling, however, was not expected through minimal religion or generalized comforting words of religious bromide, provision of which induces guilt in ministers. The settlement seems to have been needed in the relationship between the woman and her daughter. But at the first contact this could not be exposed: the daughter was distressed as she faced certain bereavement, and the mother was dying.

The simple rituals, however, seemed to be effective for these people. The minister held the dying woman's hand and gave a blessing. Both acts had the same character; they affirmed in theological terms mother and daughter and their relationship with each other in a larger context. This was not necessarily a coherent sense of God, but more likely the vast abyss which confronts human life at the ultimate boundary of death. The women felt after this, but at that moment neither they nor, most importantly, the minister could articulate this search. We note again, therefore, the requirement that the minister, even when dealing with someone who is not a member of the Church and who has no clear intention of joining, has himself to be distinctively religious and specifically Christian. The question for pastors, therefore, when engaged in such ritual activity, is how their motivation for being there and their interpretation of what they are doing are informed by the faith that they profess.

We may now begin to perceive why ritual has pastoral effectiveness in its own right. It does not have to be complicated or ritualistic and appear quasi-magical. It does, however, have to be sufficiently congruous with the minister's profession and the expectations of those asking for such pastoring that it can be used by both. Although the minister may seem to be defended from scrutiny as he performs publicly observable ritual acts, the God whom he represents is held up for examination. This suggests, therefore, that just as ministers might need to take greater care in creating and performing the ritual of worship (on which see below), so too they may need to reflect on the way that their ritual functioning, which may at times seem to them perfunctory, has a profound effect on the lives of people. That is an issue in its own right. It is also a matter of how the Church, the gospel, and therefore ultimately God, too, have a chance of being perceived.

PASTORING THROUGH WORSHIP

Pastoral care based on the resurrection involves worship. This is more than inviting people to take part in services in church. In pastoral work we enable them to bring whatever aspects of their individual and corporate lives they wish.

We can then attempt an educational process which is programmed through a liturgical act. Baptisms, weddings and funerals are instances of how people may still expect the Church to do this. Special services for groups and communities are similarly pastoral in intent and educational in form. They also show that, if it takes such ministry seriously, the Church can respond effectively and, contrary to what many people today suggest, with integrity.

This ministry feels uncomfortable, because the minister may be made to feel that he is colluding with people's most primitive expectations of him, of themselves and of God. These have a numbing quality, which feels threatening, inducing doubt and anxiety in the minister about the rightness of his role and even about the truth of his gospel. But when we are giving ritual shape to human experiences, the educational function does not have to be diminished for the process to be effective.

Example: Thomas the sceptic

The story of Thomas from John's narrative of the resurrection is illuminating (John 20.24–9). Thomas represents the person with an analytic and experimental approach to belief. He is concerned with evidence and the grounds on which he is being asked to change his mind, or be converted. He also represents those who do not wish to believe. His life would be easier without the resurrection; at least he could live with and through his sense of bereavement. But faced with an unpalatable interpretation which addresses itself exactly to his personal proclivities – 'Put your finger here' – he responds without further reflection in instant adoration, the first stage of worship. The same process is followed in pastoral ministry: we engage with people on their terms, even when there is no evident wish on their part to believe what we do; deal with the issue sensitively and educationally; and through this interpretation we move to ritual expression, which will probably be unsophisticated.

THE PASTOR'S ANXIETY

Pastoral care based on creation and resurrection, therefore, draws attention first to the minister and what he feels to be expected of him rather than to the client or penitent. It emphasizes the pastor's public roles as God-person, representative of the Church and even, especially in people's unconscious minds, purveyor of some sort of magic. It also stresses the importance of our engagement with folk religion as a genuine religious expression. We may not feel comfortable with it; indeed, we probably should not. But the resurrection will not allow the pastor to dismiss it as none of the Church's concern. Third, it directs us to the practical use of ritual and worship, in which there is no need to worry that the Christian faith seems to be betrayed.

But the fact is that we do worry. Many ministers are perturbed by these dimensions to their ministry, not least amid the many transitions that societies and the churches are today undergoing. The question is how to survive as we are caught up in this welter of deeply felt, dimly grasped, but profound experiences and associated superstitions. A seminarian recently remarked that it was all very well knowing about the person of Christ and the revealed Father, but this did not help much when confronted by devotion to the bleeding heart of Jesus. The core doctrine of the resurrection ensures, however, that the chief betrayal in such circumstances would lie less in countenancing the debased beliefs of people than in the minister's operating without sufficient regard to his own profession of Christian faith. The approach to Christian ministry is through being able to use ourselves both as what we are and what we represent for others. The clue each time is the use made of us.

If pastors are to be willing to be used, they need the model of integration in person and role that we shall most clearly see when we consider the incarnation. But they also need more – some means of holding together the complex interactions between the minister's person and role, his life and that of others, the Church and its environment, and ultimately God and the world. In other words, they need a way of dealing with the necessary undergirding of pervasive dependence without allowing it to become stultifying. The creation/resurrection sustains this side of the minister's and the Church's life. It is at the core of Christian faith, which, if explored in the light of experience and ministry, reinforces the minister in his pastoral dealings with others and in his basic calling and motivation as a Christian.

CHAPTER EIGHT

Enjoying God:
creation, resurrection and the
disciples' worship

We have noted that the twin themes of creation and new creation are not private concerns of the Church. They intersect with common human experience and general religious belief at the point of worship. This activity is not the prerogative of the believer, but is shared by many, if not most, people. If prayer, as we shall see, is a more widespread phenomenon than we usually realize, people demonstrate a worship-like stance towards an object or person more frequently than they readily admit. A worshipper bows before God, sings his praises, rehearses his mighty acts, and seeks forgiveness and renewed strength. The whole activity is typically play, having little discernible motive and no obvious purpose. Indeed, within the Christian tradition it has been reprehensible to take part in worship hoping for some reward. It is the way we accept God's invitation to share his delight in his creation. Movement in worship reminds us of this. Although liturgical movements have on the whole become ritualized, they still take place. For example, people may sit, stand or kneel; the minister may walk between stall, lectern, pulpit and altar. Offertory processions are now a central act in most Eucharists. These are the residue of the primary movement that underlies worship – the dance of all creation around God.

THE CREATION AT PLAY

In Christian worship we play with God in his creation. This sounds childish. It is not. But it should be childlike. We should distinguish this notion from the idea that worship is the play of God's creatures before their creator. That view emerges whenever worshippers are infantilized and encouraged to behave as children. This is childishness, which confirms immature dependence in such a way as to prevent development. God becomes a powerful, albeit benevolent, paternal figure as we abdicate to him what are properly our responsibilities and revert to childishness.

Playing with God is different. It allows us to give the widest range to our dreams and hopes. We receive permission as adults, struggling with the important and unimportant demands of life, to regress to an immature posture without feeling that this is untoward or, what is more important, that by so doing we deny our autonomy. In other words, looked at as a form of behaviour, worship enables participants to move through a structured regression to a dependent acknowledgement of God. Between work and rest we can face our illusions and relate them to a deliberate, conscious sense of the realities of ourselves and our life in the created order.

WORSHIP AS MANAGED REGRESSION

These remarks on Christian worship are probably familiar. But when we recognize the theological significance of dependence, worship can be revalued in the light of the process of regression.

'Regression' and 'dependence', as we have repeatedly found throughout this study, together sound disturbing. 'Regression' seems pejorative; 'dependence' does not seem appropriate to adult behaviour. When brought into a discussion of the emotional experience of worship they seem unduly cold. In addition, in a society which idolizes achievement, sophistication and individualism, any sense of surrender to dependence sounds undesirable. When, however, we deny the significance of regression, we in fact cease to develop towards that maturity which we proclaim more easily than we live.

Life consists of perpetual movement between our past and present and between our fantasies and the realities that press on us.[1] Structured or managed regression provides the way to acknowledge these facts – our necessary dependence; our fantasized worlds, which affect our decisions and behaviour; and the curiosity which makes us human. We deliberately return to and build upon the genuine foundation of the basic psychological condition with which we are created.

Folk religion, for example, persists because in some form it is necessary for human life. Its demise has often been predicted, but it does not disappear; this is because the primitive expressions and expectations which make up that mélange of belief and practice are part of the underlying nature of us all. Although such religion emphasizes assurance and thus tends to encourage a stuck dependence, in practice it always includes, in however small a way, some expectation of change. Superstitious people, for example, are not solely dealing with felt anxiety. The effort to avert danger changes the way that they relate to their environment. It is, therefore, false to contrast folk religion with 'true' religion, as if the one was seeking dependable reassurance while the other stood for exploration by independent spirits seeking change. The difference between the two concerns the nature of the change expected and the way in which dependence is acknowledged and interpreted.

Regression to dependence is not, therefore, a reversion to an infantile mentality but a movement back to aspects of our origins which continue to be vital in our adult lives. It needs to be given recognition, since it provides a major way of grasping firmly the responsibility which belongs to all of us as human beings. Worship, whatever form it takes, gives distinctive form and structure to this function of necessary regression.

Example: the substructure of worship

As a congregation assembles, a number of individuals in various states of disarray, both in themselves and in their roles, come together. One may be, for instance, a mother. She has spent the week in the turmoil of home, family and many other settings. Her life has impinged upon and been affected by many others, individuals and organizations alike. She not surprisingly feels in disarray. But that experience, however personally intense, is not hers alone; we may also view her as representing other mothers in that area and the pressures upon all in that role. By allowing her to regress in a structured fashion to a dependent state, worship may gradually release this mother from the pressures of her life, both as herself and in her roles (which coincide with the confusions of others like her, whom she unwittingly represents). She is responsible for much. But she is now freed for a while to give free rein to the childlike view of the world of fantasies and illusions which lies within her.

The focus for this dependence is ultimately God, although we should not underestimate its proximate foci – the liturgy itself, the setting, or the minister. In this regressed state, however, worshippers are offered ways of reorientating themselves towards their responsibilities in God's world. Acts of worship are not merely emotional experiences. They include specific interpretation through reading, preaching and actions. Through these, people are invited to make their personal responses, which become stages towards competent living in their many roles. The mother may reorder her life as an individual person, in role or as representative of others, as she reflects upon whatever parts of her experience are uppermost and hears the interpretations and responds to them. Finally the obvious fact: services finish. The fact of ending presses the point that regression is not a state in which adults, individuals or groups, are to become fixed.

Worship, when seen in such a light – and this is not a total explanation, but it is one neglected facet of the Church's activity – addresses crucial and problematic issues of the self and its roles. It cannot be performed without deep and critical study. Indeed it may be that ministers today need to give more attention to this aspect of their role. It is becoming a commonplace that Sunday's activity is not as significant as work from Monday to Saturday, during which pastors are most likely to deal with people individually. But any such distinction proves false. We need to think carefully about the overall process of worship. It needs more thought than merely the casual adoption of whatever order is customarily used. Movement and music alike have to be co-ordinated within that process. Interpretative skills lie not just with whatever the preacher may wish to say, but in the coherence that is evidenced in all the interpretative material, readings and sermon alike.

THIS-WORLDLY WORSHIP

When we see worship in this way we cannot promote it, or, as some might wish, dismiss it, as merely an other-worldly pursuit. It takes place at one of the cores of human life, where individual and society, personal disposition and public role, together with issues of autonomy, authority and responsible behaviour, all coincide and can therefore be examined and new interpretations be regularly absorbed in changed lives.

We may now put this practical description of worship centrally in the theological context of the creation and resurrection. At the play of worship our dependence, which derives from our creation, is harnessed to the new creation. For, as we saw, it enables us to link our rational aspects with the irrational, and to co-ordinate our purposeful striving for achievement with the dimension of our existence which is being for its own sake – play. In more familiar Christian terms, through worship our lives are redeemed as we bring into focus the way of the cross as both God's way and ours. We are also restored as, through the proclamation of the resurrection, the consummation (when God will be all in all) is momentarily glimpsed.

Northrop Frye has expressed this in another context thus:

> Now that the work ethic has settled into a better perspective, the play ethic is also coming into focus, and we can perhaps understand a bit more clearly than we could a century ago why *Othello* and *Macbeth* are called plays. Play is that for the sake of which work is done, the climactic Sabbath vision of mankind.[2]

The inner connections between work and play, spirituality, prayer and worship are thus exposed. The way to outline this now is in terms both of the dynamics of human behaviour which we have been examining and of the particular approach to these that we have been using throughout this book. Of these dependence is the most persistent – the normal or basic stance. Only if this is competently handled, therefore, can the other modes of behaviour be turned to useful ends. For example, in order to be able to fight and so achieve something, people need to feel confident that the side of them that seeks basic security – that is, dependence – is being safeguarded. If not, then they are likely to revert to this and so not be able to mobilize their fight/flight dynamic to achieve success or victory.

This is a familiar phenomenon when war looms. Individuals and groups turn to the churches to guarantee a security which they know has to be discounted if they are to give their energies to fighting. As the 'fight aspects' of people and a society are geared up for war, along with the matching panic which seeks flight, people's dependence has to be reassuringly sustained and handled. Wilfred Bion, whose seminal thinking on groups is a major foundation of this book's argument, was an original thinker. From his discovery of group process he noticed similar dynamics at work in society at large. In Great Britain, for instance, the services represented fight/flight, the Church held dependence, and the aristocracy stood for pairing.[3] But they were not stuck in those roles. In any organization or society, different groups have to adopt roles on behalf of one another so that work can be furthered. Since all of us cannot do everything, consciously but more often unconsciously, we parcel out different functions to different groups or people.

No single group or individual operates with all the dynamics at the same time. Because we are as we are as human beings, organizations become necessary and delegation (so that we can act on behalf of each other) becomes crucial. The volatile dynamics of fight/flight and the fragility of the pair are needed for achievement. They are risky and often involve pain, but we can only mobilize them when our underlying dependence is safeguarded. We have fastened these two dynamics to two Christian doctrines: pairing is linked to the incarnation and its outcome in the kingdom of God; fight/flight, that double dynamic, puts Christ on the cross and endorses that way of acting and achievement as God's. Resurrection as new creation, affirming that God is willing to acknowledge his creatures in their basic stance towards him of dependence, cannot therefore be a consequence of the incarnation and the cross. It stands at the core of the Christian profession, but most closely in relation to the creation. There God handles the underlying dynamic of his creation, which makes the others usable in distinctive ways for our salvation.

Christians have a persistent penchant for diminishing the significance of this. We sometimes make the resurrection a logical outcome of the incarnation – because Christ is the Son of God he must demonstrate this by a mighty act of power. At other times, too, we treat it as the vindication of the crucifixion – the way of the cross must be proved to be truly God's way before we can invite anyone to walk in it. But both these attitudes, or assumptions, have the effect of diminishing the intrinsic importance of these two doctrines and the intimate links which they have with common human experience. Then theological insight, as it seems, undermines pastoral ministry rather than illuminates it. Consequently pastoring is devalued and surrenders its direction and theological ground to psychotherapy or religious fundamentalism, and prayer and spirituality also lose touch with their theological roots and pastoral purpose and bewilderingly decline in significance for believers.

CHAPTER NINE

And became man: incarnation, limitation and negotiation

Today's thinking about the incarnation displays the same concern with relationships that marks our contemporary world in general. Innumerable therapists offer to assist us to get them straight. They are researched and studied. Popular literature abounds on all aspects of human relating. The internet provides opportunities to meet from all corners of the globe. In theological studies similar interest is shown. Maurice Wiles provides a typical example when he writes of salvation as 'an unbreakable relationship of loving obedience to God for which the best (though still imperfect) analogy is that of personal relationship'.[1]

RELATIONSHIPS

In everyday life people go to great lengths to find a loving relationship. They pay counsellors, the new priests of an undogmatic religion of personal attention. Yet in its pastoral ministry the Church does not seem able to use the opportunity of this ferment to make an effective link between such human relationships and the gospel interpretation of God's dealings with us. As a result it is in a bind: it speaks fluently of care and love, and tries in various ways to offer both, but it lacks a gospel of changed life with God. Something feels missing as the Christian message becomes indistinguishable from other contemporary exhortations to care for a neighbour who may or may not need that concern.

Opportunities for action multiply as horizons extend from church, through parish and society, to nation and world. But a sense of guilt accompanies these efforts to offer care and love. The greater the need seems to be, the more it looks like evidence that we, the Christians who glibly speak of God's love and ours, have in practice proved insufficiently loving.

RELATIONSHIPS AND HOPE

This preoccupation with relationships is a form of hope. The lonely individual or isolated community seeks a contact with someone else or another group through which they may find a sense of permanence in an unreliable world or temporary gratification in a joyless environment. The exact form is not for the moment important: it remains hope. Our biological motivation to reproduce underlies the feeling that, if only we can get together, things as yet unknown will be created. But relationships are more significant than this. The offspring produced are the next generation; but they are also continuing evidence of the relationship itself. They, therefore, carry aspects of the hopes in which the partners invest.

Hope in this sense arises because it is an outcome of a relationship in a context – two people, two groups, two nations. In common human experience such hope is not merely an option; it is a fundamental component of living. Accounts from any of the horrific camps and places of torture that, following the Nazi example, have so disfigured our world, confirm this. Even the existentialist writers, for all their overwhelming sense of despair, affirm the significance of hope for our human existence. When our hoping part is removed (and this is itself notoriously difficult to achieve), the result is not diminished human life but a dehumanized existence, which scarcely qualifies to be called either 'human' or 'life'.

Relationships obviously differ in intensity. They have in common however a tendency to become a focal point for the individuals concerned. They also perform a similar function for others. The stronger the sense of hope in a particular relationship, the more likely it is that the couple are expressing something on behalf of others than just themselves. One obvious instance is marriage and the pressures on it today. Half the marriages in the United States now end in divorce, and trends in Europe are similar. These pressures do not arise solely from the high expectations which the partners may have of each other, but from the anxieties that they also have to cope with which are endemic in our society. Economic problems, for example, which even governments seem unable to solve, are left to newly married couples to resolve. They have to earn enough to live on or manage the stresses brought about by unemployment, even if the nation cannot do so. And the pressure is increased by casual talk of the sanctity of marriage and of society's need for stable family life. Hope is thus invested in the couple which is greater than they can realize.

We can now begin to appreciate why partnerships – good friends, parents and children, married couples, professional associations and even national alliances – are often so fragile. Because both the partners and others invest in the hope, the disappointment and anger that results when that hope fails is out of proportion and so becomes bewildering and mystifying. Any analogy which we may draw between salvation and human relating must therefore include recognition of the way in which such a relationship enables life to be sustained by others as well as by those directly involved. The Christian minister is concerned in this way with relationships and hope. His ministry involves him with people who are already in complex ways, often hidden from him and even from them, interacting with each other. In his specifically religious activities, too, such as worship and prayer, he is establishing a connection or relationship between God and man or between this world and the next. People expect him to do this. Indeed, it is when the Church and its ministers are being most distinctively religious that their opportunities for general ministry seem to become most frequent and usable.

The Christian doctrine which connects with this dimension of human life is the incarnation. Often thought of in terms of identification – 'God with us' or 'God as one of us' – we can better focus on it as a series of different paired relationships, how they are generated and why they are sustained.

THE PAIRINGS IN THE INCARNATION

It scarcely needs stating that this doctrine is central to Christian belief. For many it is the essence of Christianity. The incarnate Christ is a central theme of worship; it is also the base on which thousands (maybe even more) serve others with charity, meeting Christ in their neighbour; theologians revert to it as a core issue of Christian theology; and whatever attempts are made to shift it from its central, but problematic, status, it persistently returns. There is no clear evidence that this state of affairs is changing or is about to change, in spite of flurries of argument, books and pamphlets. Current disputes echo ancient acrimonies. Anyone who wishes to face up to Christianity, whether as believer or interested enquirer, must confront the incarnation.

So central a doctrine is bound to cause controversy, some of it seemingly remote from ordinary belief or the practice of everyday ministry. These disputes, however, all indicate one obvious point:

wherever you turn in thinking about God incarnate, you come up against linking, or twoness. The language makes extensive use of 'and', not 'or' – God and Christ; Father and Son; fully God and fully man; or, more philosophically, time and eternity; immanence and transcendence. The thrust of the Council of Chalcedon, and most subsequent theologies of the incarnation, has been to preserve 'and'. Substitute 'or' for any one of those 'ands', and you were more likely than not to have become heretical. The four famous adverbs which refer to the union of the two natures sustain the point: 'unconfusedly, unchangeably, indivisibly, inseparably'.

God and Christ

Jesus Christ and God form a primary pair. The Gospels are unequivocal about this relationship: Jesus prays to and with God; and his disciples and others associate him with God as a prophet, a miracle-worker, or the Messiah. Whether or not this last was Jesus' own claim, the stories present a Jesus who was invited by both God and his fellow men and women to function on their behalf. On the issue of Messiahship, for example, he appears to have resisted the title. Maybe he feared misunderstanding. But perhaps, too, he was aware that the fantasy world which in common human experience is constructed around relationships is too fragile to be a means of salvation, however intensely all concerned may believe that it is. The contemporary expectation was that the link between God and the Messiah would instantly achieve the salvation of the people. So Jesus consistently reinterpreted the role of 'Messiah', allowing people to use the term but always giving it back in a changed version. The most notable instance is his response to Peter's confession. Peter cries out, 'You are the Christ.' Jesus responds in terms of the suffering Son of Man (Mark 8.27ff.). He thus resisted the natural, but deluded, investment in a pair for its own sake.

There are other pairs or twonesses: God and humankind, and God and the world, are linked through the incarnation. And there is further the partnership between the man Jesus and humankind in general. As John Robinson aptly described it, from whichever angle we approach the incarnation, it is like trying to put two billiard balls on the same spot.

The pair of God and humanity, the central point of dispute around the formula of Chalcedon, became historically the test of orthodoxy. Today it is questioned anew, although not so much because of suspicion about the quality of the arguments. There seems little more to say about them. The problem now becomes acute in a different way. It arises because the concept of humanity, which is one pole of the union of God and man in Christ, has in our age become differently problematic. The Chalcedonian approach relies upon the human term in the pair remaining reliable and accessible; at least, we have reckoned, we know what we mean by 'human', even if 'God' remains more difficult. But the human sciences have removed such apparent certainty and have thus made this orthodoxy almost impossible for many.

God and the world

The second paired relationship – God and the world – asks how universal implications can be drawn from a unique event. Or what of Christ and religious expression in non-Christian religions? All of these, when we think of an incarnation, become points of renewed controversy.

Christ and the individual

The third link – that between human beings – points us to the relationship between Jesus and the individual. Here is the evangelical challenge that Christ lives and dies for each believer. Issues of Jesus' personal identity enlarge into questions about how Christ relates to the Church and of how Christians (and for that matter others) share in his continuing work. Spirituality and sacramental theology, as well as what it means to speak of 'knowing Christ', come into focus. All of these pairings in the incarnation stir up for the Christian minister more than interesting and important questions about the content of her faith. However technical a discussion may be, the doctrine draws her to the hard issues of her everyday dealing with people – the nature of existence; why relationships occur; and how hope is to be sustained. There are major issues of theology, the day-to-day business of pastoral ministry, and the substance of Christian spirituality and prayer.

RELATIONSHIP, EXPERIENCE AND RELIGIOUS EXPERIENCE

All attempts to suggest that the incarnation is of merely historical or antiquarian interest appear to fail. Individuals from time to time may come to that conclusion for themselves, but affirmation of and controversy about the incarnation are as rife as ever. It does not go away. Belief in the incarnation demands that we grapple with difficulties. Although some resolve these dilemmas simplistically, most Christians seem willing to continue the struggle rather than to surrender the doctrine. Indeed some say that this exertion and conflict gives Christianity its identity. But there is more to it than this. Running through Christian experience, in prayer, worship and what it feels like to be called 'Christian', is regard for Jesus as one to be venerated.[2] This attitude was one mark of the emerging doctrine of the incarnation and continues, though disputed, to this day. Christianity is distinguished not only by claims about Jesus Christ but also by the worship that accompanies them.

Pastors handle people's beliefs, teach religious practice and, for many, embody the Christian tradition and so make it available to them. They, therefore, particularly need a means of holding this experiential aspect to Christian theology at the heart of their activity and thinking. Theologians tend to regard religious experience as less than reliable, and accordingly assign it little evidential value.

Pastors are also theologians, but for them, by contrast with their academic colleagues, religious experience is a crucial component in their life and ministry. Their own sense of God sustains them; they cannot claim to be God's servants without being able to give personal content to the term 'God'. Even more, as Christian ministers, their interpretations of religious experience are Christian and so embody in the here-and-now of the Church's life the process by which in history the idea of the incarnation developed. They affirm both the tradition which is described as the Christian faith and continuing experiences of God.

But that is not all. Those who are not believers, for instance, with justification expect the Church and its ministers to stand for the phenomenon of religious experience. This may be ridiculed, dismissed or queried, but that claimed experience is the point at which non-believers identify believers and so may legitimately expect to have some idea of what they are dealing with. And, of course, the converse is true for believers, who search to have their present experiences of God intensified or to acquire new ones. Religious experience is the foundation of the Church's and the pastor's life. It links belief and practice, believer and non-believer, and the welter of confused expectations from inside and outside with which the Church works.

Religious experience, therefore, has to be assigned value as a datum in our theological reflection. But it cannot be isolated from common human experience, the basic component of which is relationships. This theme confronts us when we reflect both on our ordinary human experience and on religious experience, particularly in the context of the incarnation. Relationships are not ends in themselves. Through them we construct our personal development and social life. We need, therefore, to look for the underlying processes that they involve so as to see how we might today interpret the way that God addresses us in this aspect of our life.

We now know that much of our life is lived on the basis of our earliest experiences as we resolve, repeat or reuse them. None of us begins life alone. Even the most deprived person starts life in a relationship, first with a mother but soon with other people. All such relationships are ambiguous. They include good and bad feelings alike, and these have to be dealt with. As a result, relating to another necessarily involves our projecting aspects of ourselves on to them. If we like these, we may as a result seek closer attachment to that person. If, however, we dislike those parts of ourselves, we may try to punish or dismiss them. This basic quality of human life accounts for much of the bewilderment that we so often feel in our own relationships or those which we observe between others.

At the level of our unconscious behaviour every relationship is more turbulent than we may realize. Destructive rage, for example, may dominate. This is a characteristic of our earliest experience, with which we live all our lives and with which we usually learn to cope. We are not simply driven to strong feelings of anger or anxiety by things outside us. That world interacts with our inner world of the developing self, and profound unconscious attitudes are generated.

Example: out of the mouths of babes

Small children provide the best examples of this, since they express their feelings freely. These are often more full of rage than anxious parents find comfortable, understandable or even believable. The baby seems to be living in a turbulent world from the first, even though to a large degree protected by its parents from outside pressures. The experience is one of conflict – 'either/or' rather than 'both/and'. As we mature, however, our world and our connection to it take on different patterns as we shift from 'or' to 'and' and the new problems and opportunities this offers. We generally move from rivalry to a more secure sense of identity as what had seemed threateningly destructive begins to be seen as something whole to which we can relate. From that relationship hope emerges.

This process is most prominent in two periods in our lives: first, when as a baby we begin to perceive our mother as a distinct person other than ourselves, and as someone to whom we relate rather than one on whom we depend; and second, when in a sense we repeat the procedure as part of growing up into adulthood.

A similar process can also be discerned in a group when a pairing dynamic prevails. Two people are loaded with the feelings of the rest in the hope that they will produce what is needed. This allows other members to evade responsibility for the powerful, and often painful or even destructive, feelings which they themselves need to acknowledge and make use of, if anything is to be achieved. An atmosphere of expectancy is created.

Example: hopeless hopefulness

There are churches where a shifting pattern of small groups is the usual mode of life. Here hopefulness for the inner life of the church is sustained: something is always 'going to happen' – new life, new vision, new mission. Meanwhile, a rationale as to why things do not happen is created by projecting outside the group and there locating the hindrances – the demands of living, pressure of work, financial problems in young families, and the like. The process develops its own intensity. The linking may become more specific and produce the notion of an idealized leader who is created in the mind and longed for: this person, it is believed, will bring needed resources and charisma. When such fantasies are focused in an individual, any drawbacks are ignored. Observers are often mystified that blatant weaknesses or unsuitability are overlooked. But the groups within that church continue, at least for a while, to create this desirable fantasy and avoid responsibility.

Two fundamental qualities of common human experience emerge, both of which need to be addressed in any contemporary thinking on the incarnation. First, as individuals we grow as we acknowledge and work with the sense of limitation which mature people have to recognize in themselves. From almost our earliest infancy we have to come to terms with the fact that there is both what is 'I' and what is 'not-I'. This may seem obvious, but to acknowledge that there is something other than us implies restriction. Yet every human being needs to come to terms with this limitation, the bounds to himself and his existence which in fact enable him to develop at all.

Second, people exist as persons only when they negotiate with one another. There is no self-sufficient individual life. Throughout our lives we live by accepting the limitations to ourselves and to others. These make it possible in practice for us to have anything to do with each other and so to enter into relationships. Human relationships, therefore, can never be simple. To speak casually of 'relate' and its associated ideas, as preachers and pastors are inclined to do, may obliterate this range of inevitable complications and so give people a false sense of themselves, of their neighbour, and, therefore, ultimately also of God.

LIMITATION AND NEGOTIATION

Relationships are full of excitement and feelings of one sort or another. By contrast 'limitation' and 'negotiation' sound cold and formal. But these two words refer to fundamental aspects of human life which both the pastor, who tries to embody the model of the incarnation, and the theologian, who offers ways of interpreting it, need to explore in order to speak in our present age.

Limitation

Limitation is essential for growth. As we develop, we progressively become aware of ourselves ('I') by distinguishing this from what is other ('not-I'). But the individual does not do this in isolation. Even ignoring the period of gestation, we can see that our earliest moments of life are lived in the unit of mother/child. We are not self-sufficient. So the growth of the self is a continuing process of discovering what is both I and not-I. We begin to recognize limitations to our selves or, as we might call them, 'boundaries'. We then use them as the means by which we assert our individuality.

For example, when we are newly born our first perceptions are probably of near-fusion with our mother's breast. Mother and child are closely knit and the boundaries around two individuals are blurred. Growth, however, depends upon our progressively distinguishing our self from that breast, getting the boundaries clearer, until we (both child and mother) generate a relationship.

Negotiation

We become more aware of ourselves when we discover the second vital feature of life together. Once disabused of a sense of fusion, we have to devise ways of staying in touch with others. The outcome is our second chief characteristic – negotiation. This is founded on mature recognition of others. We learn that life is made up of relationships that we negotiate with others. We discover how we are related to complex, dimly felt but important, networks of human institutions, like families. So, for example, a child first negotiates with its mother through demand and response. The early words of 'I want' lead to the familiar ploys of child and mother, and the struggles begin. But the child's world is not confined to its mother. There are other people, such as a father, relatives and friends, not to mention animals. The physical world impinges. And running through all these there is the substructure of connections and associations in which the adults who inhabit the child's world are caught up.

At an early stage, for example, a child may experience his mother's behaviour as irrational and incomprehensible. Her responses to the child may not feel congruent with his demand or he may not be able to make sense of her attitude towards him in terms of his own perception of the world at that moment. But this confusing experience also makes him aware of that wider world of feelings and influences, which is greater than his immediate environment, to which he contributes and with which he will have to deal throughout his life.

THE INTENSITY OF HALF-BELIEF

Limitation and negotiation are also crucial in religious experience. The categories of 'I–Thou' and 'I–It' are usually taken as clarifying those distinctions between persons and things, or between the personal and the impersonal worlds. Both are necessary for religious experience. But a more important issue is the assumption behind them that difference, and hence the need to manage limitation, is essential for life.

Intense religious experience, such as that of the mystic, might seem to have little to do with limitation. It implies a loss of the self in oneness with God. But even this experience is only possible in so far as God and man remain distinguishable. The most profound mystical moments, when the mystic claims fusion with God, preserve this distinction by being temporary. There is no permanent mystical state. The intense quality of such experiences, which momentarily blur human individuality, is compensated for by their short duration. It is not the experience itself which cannot be tolerated; it is the loss of boundaries, or failure of our needed limitation, which implies death.

For most people, however, religious experience is less intense and more provisional than this. The half-believer often has a wistful longing for the full-blooded belief of which he or she now feels incapable. Yet they are unable to abandon a belief which will not let them go; they live permanently oppressed by a 'forgotten dream'. Others discern, behind the low level of religious activity in Great Britain since 1945, many who believe without belonging.

Ministers spend much time with such people, and this experience seems at least as common as (and is probably even more so than) that of the religiously intense. Hovering between belief and unbelief, the Christian half-believer is sustained by a twofold awareness: a sense of some sort of God, albeit vague and indeterminate, and a recognition that the way of Jesus is important and admirable. By this twofold stance the half-believer identifies himself: there is limitation, by virtue of his capacity to believe in comparison with the wish to believe; and negotiation, since the relationship between the half-believer and his longed-for God and admired Jesus has constantly to be negotiated in the light of this limited capacity for belief. The two basic themes of human life, therefore, limitation and negotiation, re-emerge in a familiar religious experience.

Religious experience, whether intense or fragile, points to limitation and negotiation. Both demand that some disjunction between the believer and God is preserved, as is confirmed by the doctrine of the incarnation. The half-believer's experience, however, further demonstrates an important point for this doctrine. For it is given an explicitly Christian orientation by preserving a distinction between God and Jesus. However intimate the connection may be, a distinction (or, we might say, a limitation, so that negotiation can occur) is essential if the religious experience of the half-believer is to be possible. So this experiential indicator directs us to the classic core of incarnational theology, but bases it on a form of religious experience which is a specific instance of common human experience.

Whether we begin with the common human experience of infancy and growth, or start with specifically religious experience, the outcome is the same. By either route we reach the complementary ideas of limitation and negotiation. Our experience of limitation is that it enables us to be sufficiently aware of our own selves that we can approach and be approached by others. This process is about drawing boundaries so that we can identify ourselves and be identified by others – the basis of all relationships.

The complementary notion is that of negotiation. Individuals and groups use boundaries, as they become aware of them, as points for negotiation with others and with the world, and so they create new things. This newness may be personal – our growth – or it may belong to us and to others as together people come to a renewed perspective on some aspect of our world. But such developments come about only as we discern our boundaries, whether as individuals, groups or even societies, and so can confidently negotiate with others. It is as governments and world leaders become aware of the boundaries to themselves, to their primary groups and, in the case of particularly effective politicians, boundaries to their nation that there is any hope for the work of diplomacy.

This way of seeing human life and behaviour is emerging in the present age as people explore what it means to be human. The question for the pastor as theologian, however, is critical: given this range of human behaviour, much of it drawing the minister's attention to the unconscious dimensions of life, how can we today conceive of and speak about God encountering us? If we cannot address this question, then we have found part of human life from which, wittingly or not, the claims of God have been excluded. Such a conclusion, however, is inconceivable for the believer. What ideas about the incarnation, therefore, may emerge when we give specific attention to these understandings of our human life and of the pastor's involvement with it? This question may involve neglecting some other no less useful themes. For the pastor, however, such selection is essential. We have to discover what happens to the Christian notion of the incarnation when we base our thinking upon the data which the pastor continually encounters via common human experience and specific religious experience alike.

INCARNATION, LIMITATION AND NEGOTIATION

When we use the categories of limitation and negotiation, we are freed from the constraints which usually dominate discussion about the incarnation. Traditionally these have concerned identity.

But by emphasizing differences (limitation) and how they are employed (negotiation), we may find a way of holding together and illuminating our faith in the incarnation and our pastoral practice deriving from it.

Limitation

Every approach to the incarnation has to grapple with limitation. Kenotic[3] theories may in themselves be inadequate, but their emphasis on self-emptying and surrender (what we could call 'limitation') lies at the heart of all reflection on the incarnation. If we pursue the idea of limitation using common human experience as our reference, we first note that it is essential for growth and development. In this light it is neither constricting nor diminishing. It describes the way in which we acquire and consolidate the boundaries by which we define ourselves in relation to others. From this sense of limitation the centre of attention becomes not our personal inner life but how we act with others in various settings – our roles. There is no absolute distinction between person and role, but it is one worth making as a help towards clarity in thinking about the significance of limitation for the incarnation.

Example: a growing girl

Take, for example, a normally growing girl. We are not usually very concerned to diagnose her inner motivations and how they may or may not be expressed. The important point is the way in which, as a child in relation to different contexts – mother, father, social setting and so on – she is being defined and defining who she is. Her inner life is highly relevant, but we do not have to become preoccupied with it and with data from it, to which we have little or no access. In most circumstances we can know enough about her and her development through how she behaves and what she does. This gives us sufficient grounds on which to make judgements and to respond to her.

The same principle applies to our theological reflection on Jesus Christ. We live without information about him, particularly his inner life and motivations. These will always be questionable and be an area in which the faithful projectively explore their faith. This, as we saw in our examination of the atonement, is not illegitimate behaviour; it is precisely God's intention in making himself vulnerable in this way. Our inevitable ignorance, however, is not worrisome. Jesus' public self, as presented in the stories of the Gospels, is sufficient for us to begin to reflect on the significance of God's use of that limitation which is basic to all human experience. The debate about what may be known of Jesus of Nazareth continues. Underlying it is the long-standing argument over the connection between the man of Nazareth and what believers confess about him, sometimes called the debate between 'the Jesus of history' and 'the Christ of faith'. This distinction, however, although significant in biblical and theological studies, seems to have had little impact on the Church at large. Ministers have tried to use it in teaching their congregations, but there are few signs of its having taken root there. Current liturgical revisions do not appear to recognize it. The concepts of limitation and boundaries, however, suggest why this may be so and take us further into an important area for incarnational thinking.

The distinction between the Jesus of history and the Christ of faith is not something outside of us which we can debate. Thus it is not first about Jesus, but it directs attention to the negotiation which we each continually make between who we are (our inner selves) and what we are (ourselves as seen and used by others). We can describe this more tersely as the continuing negotiations between our person (who we are) and our various roles (what we are).

The word 'role' carries unfortunate overtones of acting or playing. It may suggest a mask which can be taken up or laid down at will. In religious contexts this may imply hypocrisy: if I am playing a role, I am not myself acting with integrity. But the term is used here more precisely, not of something assumed or laid down but of a function which is performed in relation to a task. This, as it stands, is a little cryptic. It needs explaining, and the best way to do that is through an illustration.

Example: the role of father

Father's 'role' is a function of a family; that of priest is a function of the Church. Without 'family' – mother and child – 'father' has little or no meaning; similarly, without 'Church', however we interpret that large term, we cannot understand 'priest'. But no role is simple. Because it is a function it will be affected by what an organization – say, a family or a church – is doing. In addition, we all simultaneously occupy several roles in life, which leads to conflict between them.

The key point, however, is that, whatever the role, it always has to be negotiated. My inner motivation, why I have elected, say, to be a parent or a priest, can be explored, but it remains a concern which I may or may not care to share. As roles, however, 'father' or 'priest' are different. They are not private to me but are created through negotiation with others as they make their assumptions about me and explore what I may represent for them. I may have a view of my role as parent, but I do not determine it; it can only be thought of in relation to others, first the immediate family and then the wider range of a cultural setting and its assumptions about parenthood. The same is true of 'priest' and of any other role. Because it is negotiated with others, its chief mark is that it is available for public scrutiny as against the privacy of the person.

Boundaries

Such scrutiny, however, cannot be done from a distance. It brings people together and invites them to test the points at which their lives, beliefs and fantasies impinge on one another. The term which we have already used, 'boundary', now comes into play to describe these points of scrutiny.

When two people, groups or organizations do anything together, they work with a series of perceptions of themselves and each other. A church, for example, may think of itself as the embodiment of God's love in a place; those to whom it turns, however, may see it as the place in which to locate their fear of death and the unknown. This does not mean that these groups cannot meet. But the church's sense of its boundary, what it thinks it stands for to other people, and other people's sense of their boundary in relation to that church, need to be appreciated. This way of drawing boundaries follows when we recognize limitation as one way by which we define ourselves and are defined by others.

A church, for instance, cannot be just what it likes to think it is; it is limited to some extent to what it is also allowed to be by others. We all experience this. Today it is frequently called a communication problem. The concept of a boundary, however, can help us focus on the issue as it is, rather than leap too quickly into explanation. It helps to discern the interface between what I think I am and what other people make me or wish me to be, where my person and roles coincide.

Pastors regularly work in this area as they and those with whom they minister negotiate the distance between their self-image as a

Christian minister and people's assumptions about them as, say, a holy person or God-man. Neither our own definition from within nor the view of others alone constitutes the role: it is created and becomes useful through that negotiation which becomes possible when the importance of limitation (boundaries) is recognized. Without this, we might say, there is no pastor, but only one person's fantasies about himself and a set of images held by others. Boundaries are therefore a means to personal development and to collaborative endeavour. They are creative, and limitation is, paradoxically, not limiting.

We should note, however, that, although the term 'limitation' (and its variants) has a long history in reflection on the incarnation, I am proposing it here and discussing it within a specific context. It directs us to accessible material and the idea of role rather than any preoccupation with questions of inner drives or motivation. For the moment three points need to be held in mind.

First, 'limitation' (and the associated idea of 'boundary') draws attention to the important fact that difference and separation are the only means that human beings possess for establishing relationships. The idea of knowing someone is more complex and profound than is sometimes realized. Limitation as a concept offers us a way of sustaining the idea of relationship at the centre of our thinking without slipping into fantasies about what we know of ourselves and of others.

Second, the notion makes use of the distinction between person and role, thus emphasizing the way that people become available to one another and consequently vulnerable to mutual scrutiny. Whatever we may be in ourselves ('I' or 'Jesus of Nazareth'), this is not separable from whatever we are in relation to others ('my roles' or 'the Christ of faith'). Thus two traditional themes of the doctrine of the incarnation – God's accessibility and vulnerability – emerge once again. But now from a new perspective: they are not the results of some divine choice but are necessary conditions of any relationship, whether between God and man, or Jesus and God, or man and man, or Jesus and his developing self.

Third, questions of the unconscious world, which we have already seen to be so significant for people today and consequently for theology, are not confined to a fruitless attempt to explore and even analyse Jesus' psychological make-up. They are involved in interrelation, as seen in the many pairs of this doctrine, and in the notion of role, by which people (including Jesus Christ) become available for scrutiny.

Negotiation

Negotiation is more briefly described. Since the kernel of the doctrine of the incarnation is a series of pairs, Jesus Christ cannot be considered except in terms of them. A relationship between him and God is basic. It is presumed, for example, by the stories of Jesus at prayer and in particular the cries from the cross. He is also defined through significant interchanges with other people. The relationship between Jesus and his neighbour, whoever that is at any moment, is a central theme in the Gospels, and was rapidly picked up by the early Church. These two negotiations – with God and the neighbour – have also proved crucial in the believer's experience down the ages, and they remain so. Christians claim that Jesus is an access point to God. His dealings with God, therefore, are obviously vital. But negotiation between Jesus and his neighbour is also essential, because the believer himself is one such neighbour. For us to have access to God through Jesus Christ we need both these links – Jesus and God, Jesus and neighbour.

There is, however, a third, but more complicated, link in our human lives which must also find a place in any doctrine of the incarnation – that between the self and the developing self. As we grow we renegotiate within ourselves what we were and what we are becoming. The loss of innocence is one example of this. Something happens to us and, as a result, we have to negotiate a shift from what we formerly were, innocent and ignorant, to what we now are, knowledgeable but different, even corrupted. If we do not manage such transitions, we can get stuck either in the process itself or in a fantasized former state, pretending that nothing has happened. Every transition involves negotiation. We abandon one state or attitude as we take up a new one. Usually this happens without our realizing it. But on reflection we may discover what took place and find ourselves unexpectedly wistful. Any gain is accompanied by a sense of irreplaceable loss.

Example: Jesus' development

This aspect of our ordinary experience invites us to reflect upon Jesus' self-consciousness in a new way. We have already noted that we can never know specific details about this. But neither can we discount the development in his life that is presented in the Gospel writers' accounts and in the early theological reflections upon these. Each Gospel from its own perspective presents a Jesus who in his adult behaviour shows signs of growth like any human person. St Mark, for example, describes the beginnings of his ministry as tentative. Jesus indiscriminately heals people and then retires to pray. Against the disciples' pressure he refuses to return, but moves on with a more clearly stated task: 'I have to proclaim my message . . . That is why I came' (Mark 1.38). The next healing indicates this change. It is specifically set in the social and religious context of the day: Jesus sends the cured leper to conform to the law's requirements. But in this new law-confirming stance we can foresee the conflict with the authorities which will finally crucify him.

This type of shift from first enthusiastic encounters to more mature ministry is not peculiar to Jesus. It is an instance of that common human experience of having to struggle at every moment with who we are and the transition into what we are becoming. This is, notoriously, the distinctive problem of adolescence; nevertheless it affects us throughout our lives. Although, therefore, Jesus' negotiation between his self and developing self must remain hidden, the idea that he, like us, was caught up in it is necessary. While the details of such development are unknowable, it does not follow that the fact cannot be acknowledged.

The themes of limitation and negotiation are integral to any contemporary reflection on the incarnation. They are also ways of approaching the question of transference, a key mode by which we relate to one another. During an analysis the boundaries within which transference is going to be risked are carefully defined because of the powerful material that is likely to be unlocked. They are also drawn in everyday life, although by no means so precisely. Sometimes such boundaries are sanctioned by convention. For example, confidentiality is generally ascribed to the religious role of the priest in the confessional. This enables the priest/penitent relationship to be used transferentially for that between God and the penitent.

Since, however, such transference is a facet of common human experience, especially when a pair is concerned, the crucial question for the pastor as theologian is how God engages with us at this level. That, theologically, is where the incarnation comes in. We have noted how fundamental pairings are to all human life and experience. We now need to bring the concepts of limitation and negotiation, and the particular way that they come together in the idea of transference, to bear on the way that we might think of the incarnation, in the context of our pastoral practice and Christian discipleship.

Incarnation

Life is composed of a series of relationships which can neither be segmented into unconnected pairs nor blurred into an undifferentiated whole. Transference demonstrates that we regularly shift perspectives between different relationships as a way of bringing about change. The result is some new possibility and way of living – that is, hope. Thus someone, a person who is not my father, can be sufficiently 'father' for me to deal with some unresolved issue in my life involving myself and my relationship with others. This does not necessarily come about through formal treatment; it is a facet, usually unrecognized, of everyday living.

The doctrine of the incarnation is precisely about this question, inviting us to see how various relationships can be opened up, given new dimensions and explored through one another. For instance, it invites us to enlarge our perspective on the perennial social problem of how I live with my neighbour by transferentially using my relationship with God. In this, through some religious activity – worship or prayer – God can become 'neighbour' and thus invite us to deal with an aspect of ourselves which may need opening up and profound change. Or, as is more familiar to Christians, if I wish to become clearer about my relationship with God and his with me, I am invited to do this by first exploring what is occurring in my relationship with my neighbour. These are examples of the way that transference permeates the Christian tradition.

The criterion which applies to transference, whether in a specific or generalized sense, is 'usability'. This is not the same as usefulness, but describes the capacity of someone or something to be employed by others as a means of testing the value of something. It refers to how accessible a relationship can become to those involved so that it can be used for more than its own immediate and obvious ends.

For example, a pastor may be approached for counsel. But in addition to what he says, an important factor in the meeting is his 'usability'. This describes his willingness to accept that he may also (and even more importantly) be being used by the other to assign importance to the problem itself. He or she is thus immediately assured that what is concerning them matters. There is nothing that the minister can do about this; it is a function of his usability alongside whatever usefulness he may provide in the actual counselling.

Here we reach the heart of the incarnation. The theme of God becoming 'one with us' is less important than his action in being deliberately caught up in our world of transference, where the criterion is not association (being with) but availability (being used). For God to be with us (Emmanuel) becomes not just identification with us. It is more profound: God's chosen criterion by which he is to be judged is the extent of his availability to be used by his creatures. This is because transference is using one relationship (usually an intimate and intense one) in such a way as to allow new experience of another.

But how might God offer such usability? And what is the significance of the incarnation for it? In our everyday experience of transference, talk, although important, is never enough. Although the experience of transference is one of feeling, this is often too deep to be articulated or too vague to be spoken clearly. These feelings cry out for interpretation. And this, too, gives us a clue about the incarnation. For the process of interpretation is one of joining in usability. The interpreter, when caught up in transference, does not provide the answer or the solution to someone's problem. He is at the time part of the problem. Together, however, the pair can seek to clarify what the transference is about, to expose at least some of the connection implicit in it, and then invite action in response.

In our dealings with God verbal interpretations of our lives are not even available. People who stress the present word of God in Scripture do not on the whole argue that it is specifically directed to individual moments. Such use has a taint of magic. With him interpretation is, therefore, as in everyday experience, always more than words. God's interpretative stance, as we join him in the various transferences by which we live, lies in the model of activity which he offers in the incarnation of Jesus Christ. This is why Jesus Christ can be called 'the word of God', or, as a result of our present discussion, 'God's interpretation'. This Jesus, like any other person, is not solely identified from within but comes to be as boundaries are negotiated. This also makes him, like any other person, vulnerable. But in our everyday world of transference he becomes usable, that is, he becomes God.

The gospel, therefore, does not offer understanding, that is, certain knowledge of human life, its hopes and fears, its dilemmas and ambiguities. Although it is at times proclaimed as if it did, this is to pretend to have dealt with, and so, by implication, to have dispensed with, something basic to our lives. The result is that people are dehumanized and their lives devalued – something to which religion is occasionally prone. The gospel of God incarnate offers a model for interpreting the basic experiences of every human life, which is lived in relationship and therefore is dominated by transference.

Seen this way, the incarnation is not a doctrine about God's being one with us; nor does it feed our aspirations to become one with God. Incarnation is God's statement of his willingness to be used in the confused human dynamics of transference. The two primary components of our human development, limitation and negotiation, appear as aspects of God's life too. In Jesus, however, we see them transformed as the priority that we tend to assign to personal growth is consciously subordinated to activity in role. Jesus, like any of us, displays the self-orientated aspects of our common human experience but consistently deploys them on behalf of others – God and his neighbour.

For example, each Gospel portrays him becoming aware, as he moves towards the passion, that, while he remains responsible for his own actions, he is undertaking them on God's behalf. The struggle in Gethsemane is a specific instance, but the same theme appears in the presentations of Jesus' death: the paradox of holding control of events by surrendering it. Acting fully on his own authority but exercising it on behalf of others is the theme throughout his ministry. This brings him into conflict with some and makes him a source of wonder to others. The fragility of any pair – in this case those between Jesus and God and Jesus and his neighbour – is not denied. On the contrary, our attention is consistently drawn to it and it is acted upon, until ultimately it is confirmed in the cry of dereliction from the cross.

When we reflect on the incarnation we are considering material that is not easily accessible. This sometimes leads to theorizing which does not impinge on ordinary life and which the pastor accordingly rejects or ignores. But underlying both the stance suggested here and the minister's experience is the obvious point that the only evidence available to us about people's inner lives or of what is going on in any relationship is public behaviour. Hypotheses about people can be based only on what we can scrutinize. In the case of the incarnation the evidence for the pairings that we have discerned lies both in the handed-on stories about Jesus and in the commitment of believers to faith in him.

DIFFERENCES AT WORK

These pairings can each be examined using the critical test of relationships: how differences are made to work and, more importantly, for whom. First, there is the relation between God and Christ, as displayed in Jesus' teaching and ministry. This proves secure enough to resist pressure to separate his activity from that of God. Jesus did not contest God's responsibility for his world nor did he shirk his own. It is perhaps because of this strong sense of his own responsibility, and therefore authority, that he gives short shrift to hypocrites, those who publicly aspire to responsibility without taking it, thus displacing it on to others.

Second, when we consider Jesus in relation to his neighbour, whoever this is at any moment, we find as a mark of his ministry that no person has to be diminished in order to encounter Jesus. They are able to become something for one another, and so the differences between them may become usable. Thus the simple and the wise, the strong and the weak alike are recognized and affirmed for what they are. They are offered new chances, but are not abused by being 'understood'. Instead they are caught up in the necessarily joint activity of interpretation.

Third, the external pressure upon the inner life of Jesus, between his person and the several roles which he occupies and with which he struggles, seems not to have exposed any weakness. His relationship with himself continues integrated and provides that assurance of reliability (responding to our inevitable dependence) which is a precondition of work at issues of transference. Thus to whichever pairing we turn, each remains intact enough for people, both then and now, to use it. It can be a model which they can embody in themselves and their own life and as a reference by which to interpret this life in various relationships.

THE CRITERION OF 'USABILITY'

This is why the incarnation remains central to Christian faith. The various theological arguments have their days. But functionally they represent the intellectual effort necessary to sustain a working model. Ministers inevitably find practical questions paramount. They are, however, no less concerned with questions of truth. But theirs is the additional nagging question: Why does the incarnation matter for these people, believers and unbelievers, with whom I live and work?

The temptation is on the one hand to isolate the theological problems of the incarnation, while on the other hand trying to sustain the proclamation of God with us and the Church's worship of this Christ. Succumbing to this, however, the pastor, and eventually the Church, will split what is crucially held together in the doctrine of the incarnation. For where there are pairs, division is always likely to occur. 'And' is at risk of becoming 'or'. We have noted that pairs in this doctrine go beyond those on which theologians customarily focus. They are not only about the relation between Godhead and manhood in Jesus Christ, but as they are used they extend to every area of human life through the underlying issue of relationship. The focus thus becomes less on the person of Jesus Christ, significant as that is, than on the model of divine activity which is offered for us, which may be summed up as 'the criterion of usability' (see the discussion of 'usability' on pages 133–4).

Yet this does not make theological criteria merely pragmatic. The incarnation turns out to be what historically it has been confessed to be – God's ultimate invitation to his creatures to explore him, ourselves and our neighbours. Limitation, negotiation and transference are confirmed as God's way of enhancing his usability for all mankind. When we see this, the remarkable presentation of Jesus in the Fourth Gospel is illuminated:

[I pray] that they may be one. As you, Father, are in me and I in you, may they also be in us, so that the world may believe that you sent me. I in them and you in me, that they may be made perfectly one; that the world may know that you sent me and loved them, as you loved me. (John 17.21–3)

This meditation on the incarnation, put in the mouth of the incarnate one himself, directs us precisely to the series of pairs that we have discerned. Every relationship discloses itself in what it produces. This frequently causes embarrassment, as, for example, when parents see themselves in unacceptable aspects of their children. Traditional sayings like 'He's a chip off the old block' or gospel proverbs like 'You shall know them by their fruits' have been confirmed and to some extent expounded by contemporary behavioural study. The pairings in the incarnation are no exception.

INCARNATION AND THE KINGDOM OF GOD

Either the Christian Church or the Holy Spirit might be thought of as outcomes of the pair of God and Jesus Christ in the incarnation. The Church may not be an extension of the incarnation, but it exists and lives by that model. The Holy Spirit, according to the Western creed, 'proceeds from the Father and the Son'. However, the idea that best sums up the outcome of the incarnation is the kingdom of God.

The kingdom is not identical with the Church. That implicit triumphalism has been done away with, not least in the humiliating experience of the Church during the twentieth century. But a connection between the life and work of the Church and God's activity, which we call 'the kingdom of God', is indisputable. Similarly with the Spirit. A major recovery in recent times has been the demanding future dimension of the Spirit. He disrupts any individual or church which claims present completeness. But this experience of the Spirit firmly links it with that orientation towards the future which is found in the concept of the kingdom of God.

The idea of 'the kingdom of God' is contested, but some consistent themes emerge. It cannot be located, but represents the movement of God's activity in which he invites men and women to share. The kingdom is better regarded as opportunity than as event or happening. To be 'not far from the kingdom' (Mark 12.34) is to begin to participate with God, even if unwittingly, and so become an occasion for unexpected divine working. But God's opportunity does not begin with Jesus and his proclamation of the kingdom. Jesus affirms what had hitherto been perceived as God's ways of acting by demonstrating a new style to it. The chief difference lies in the way in which God's work now becomes more open to human scrutiny.

The revelation focused through Jesus invites us to look anew at God and ourselves. When we are sensitive to God in his creation we employ our conscious selves through reflection and intellectual apprehension and exploration, or through our aesthetic response to music, art or literature. These familiar aspects of religious life, however, also involve our unconscious selves, although necessarily we are unaware of this. Yet now we have been alerted to our unconscious world and its significance, as well as to the ways in which conscious and unconscious behaviour mesh. The question is no longer 'Does God engage with our unconscious?' but, 'How can we think about his encounter with that aspect of ourselves?'

The doctrine of the incarnation, through its emphasis on pairs and their usability, affirms that God is involved with our most fundamental human aspects. God's new quality of availability in the incarnation lies in the way in which he now offers for scrutiny a specific and intimate pair, God and Christ. There he invites us, using the transference which marks our human life, to test and discover for ourselves the two great human issues of relationship – that which we have with God and that which we share with our neighbour. These have always been part of humankind's religious quest and remain fundamental.

The distinctively Christian contribution is that God enables these two basic relationships to be explored through his use of a third – the integrating connection that God makes with himself. How this is kept alive and present to believers and through them to others is exactly the theme of the kingdom. The model of divine activity in the incarnation cannot be left in the past history of Jesus. Teaching, preaching and pastoral practice which do this fall under the judgement of God's continuing activity. People no longer live between present and past alone. The Christian gospel of the incarnation and the kingdom explicitly adds the dimension of the future.

THE KINGDOM AND THE FUTURE

This idea affects the way in which the basic issue of transference is understood. Both in the structured analytic context and informally throughout human life, transferences are usually explored between past and present, what we have been and now are. But the model of the incarnation, as this is taken up and continued in the kingdom of God, shifts the scale to one between present and future. Our life is interpreted primarily in relation to what we are, the roles we at present occupy and struggle to fulfil, and what is necessarily unknown, but impinges on our present life – the future. This gospel is founded upon the premise that no one has to be other than they now are in order to come to be someone new.

There is inevitably ambiguity when we think about present and future together. But this brings us back to the question of relationship and salvation with which we began this chapter. This ambiguous sense is a mark of salvation: it is an immediate experience of the here-and-now and includes the uncertainty that arises from its having a future aspect. When two people or groups pair, what is happening in the present is always significant in itself. But every such relationship also bears hope and so carries implications for the future.

But the trouble with hope is that the moment it is realized it ceases to be hope. When this happens a relationship may come under unbearable stress, since we sustain our relationships to some extent by this unrealized, and often unrealizable, hope. Marital breakdown, for instance, can often be attributed to the way that the partners did not work between their present, the coming together and investment in each other, and the future, the hope which they were generating and its connection with reality. When such fantasized hope dominates, present activity becomes unrealistic. And this experience is not the prerogative of intimate relations. In religion, for example, this is the point at which religion declines into delusion.[4]

SALVATION

The salvation which the incarnation offers is new experiences and perceptions of ourselves and God, and consequently of our neighbour and the world. This comes about as we use the opportunities for interpretation that God provides in the various pairings with which we are confronted. We are invited to discover new perspectives on every relationship, however secure and familiar or novel and fragile, by using other relationships which God offers us, most notably his own exposed relationship with Christ.

This process is also suffused with hope. It involves our religious longings, which we express as a wistful desire for continuity. The relationship with God in Christ saves because God invests not in that relationship itself but in the dynamic of pairing which underlies human existence and in the first place generates all relationships. The incarnation is God's public testimony to this. It is not just a series of complex interrelations within the Godhead and between God and humankind. It is God's vulnerable investment of himself in one of the bases of human life as he has created it – the pair.

Salvation, therefore, cannot be described simply as a relationship. It affects our lives more deeply than that. The pastor's concern with salvation brings together two crucial factors: first, the series of relationships which are held within the doctrine of the incarnation and which issue in the kingdom of God; second, the fact that in that incarnation God endorses all these essential human dynamics. Sometimes by comparison with other work –

counselling in particular – the pastor's involvement with people seems to be shallow. It is not; it is different. Pastoring brings together something profound about humankind and aspects of the essence of God himself.

Example: the Messiah

Jesus does not reject the roles that are thrust upon him – teacher, healer or Messiah. He is willing to be usable so that he can make these attributed roles usable by others. Peter in the confession at Caesarea Philippi (Mark 8.27f.) received one such powerful response to his presuppositions about himself and Jesus and about God and the Messiah. He was given a chance to reinterpret his life and future. It is also notable how, almost without exception, the future consequences of these encounters are acknowledged.

THE FUTURE IMPERATIVE OF THE KINGDOM

This tendency, which runs through Jesus' ministry, becomes the norm in the encounters in the passion story. Jesus engages in ministry with people between their present and the future; there is little about pasts, and when they do arise, they are dealt with in so far as they have created a present from which the person concerned has to find a new life. When, for example, Jesus heals lepers he deals with them as here-and-now sufferers without getting into debate about the origins of their sickness.

In the Fourth Gospel, where these aspects of Jesus' ministry are expounded in a condensed fashion, the writer explicitly tells a story about Jesus dealing peremptorily with that question. To the disciples' asking, 'Did this blind man or his parents sin?', Jesus replies that neither did. The man is to be given new life by beginning now: 'He was born blind so that the works of God might be demonstrated in him.' It was not God's intention to make this man an example, but as a result of his being blind this moment is the one to be grasped for interpretation for the benefit of the man, his parents, the disciples, the bystanders, and Jesus himself (John 9.1–3).

We later find the same process recounted in the life of St Paul. His relationship to God was initially changed on the Damascus road by his vision. This, however, became usable by Paul only after Ananias had joined him in interpreting it. He used the neighbour-to-neighbour relationship, instantly establishing a here-and-now link with Saul, as the way for him to begin to grasp his own new relationship with God. Ananias greeted him, touching and addressing him in the language of a new relationship – 'Brother Saul' (Acts 9.17). Ananias became for Paul a usable embodiment of that Christ with whom he had had his original striking meeting.

This is an instance of the everyday transference that we have considered earlier. Later, in Romans, Paul was to expound how man's relation with God is exposed for examination by the relationship between Christ and God. And in Romans 7 he goes on to explore how that most difficult relationship, the one between our self and our developing selves, can be unravelled for salvation through other relationships, notably that between the Christian and Christ.

Example: a marriage problem

We can derive a further example of the way in which the nature of the kingdom of God as the outcome of the pairs in the incarnation is demonstrated from everyday pastoral ministry. A man comes with a problem about his marriage. If the minister avoids being pulled into a detailed examination of the past, he or she can free that person to examine his relationship to his wife, at least a little, through his relationship to the minister. He can work on what seems to be happening between his visitor and his own role of, say, man of God (however that is fantasized) and bearer of hope or ideals or assurance.

If he can have some sense of the generalized transference that is being employed, two points follow. First, he can use his own transferences to his model of God in Christ, to help him clarify what is being asked of him. And, second, he can offer interpretation to the other about the several relationships which constitute his marriage. The question in such an encounter is not just what has happened; what might happen and what can be expected to happen are significant ingredients. The minister's perspective and ministry are different from the retrospective stance of the counsellor or analyst, even though insights derived from their approaches to human beings will inform pastoral ministry. Christian ministry, like the kingdom of God, oscillates between present and future.

CONCLUSION

We can begin to see, therefore, that the doctrine of the incarnation is firmly located both in common human experience and in the particular experience which pastors themselves acquire through their ministering with people. This setting is significant for any theology which seeks to prosper in the contemporary world. Thinking about the incarnation must take account of that vast area of human behaviour which now goes under the general heading of our unconscious life. We have seen that there are ways of thinking about it. Theologians would have to take them further in integrating these experiential issues with the persistent philosophical questions. But for the working pastor the important point is to be able to see that the incarnation of God in Jesus Christ is a specific act through which God engages not just generally with this world but specifically with the unconscious dimension of human life. The clue to this lies in the several pairings which give us both points to latch on to in our thinking about the ramifications of orthodox doctrine and a way into the contemporary theory of the unconscious life of individuals and of groups.

In their pastoral care ministers of the incarnation use a model of activity which embodies this divine, kingdom-like affirmation of the present in the context of the future. They hold together the various realities about human beings that continue to be discovered and the point of interpretation offered for all these relations by this distinctive Christian belief. Neither human beings nor their relationships are fixed enough to become simple, secure reference-points. Everything is more fluid than maybe we had realized; but it does not follow that it is chaotic. Nevertheless, behind the credal confession 'and was made man', there now appear more powerful dynamics and complications than have hitherto troubled the theologians. But the pastor daily lives with these. Now, therefore, we must ask what effect such a perspective may have upon pastoral ministry.

CHAPTER TEN

God is with us:
incarnation and pastoral care

Christian ministers often offer care to individuals and groups in terms of identifying with them. They are inclined to believe that they should (and can) stand where people stand, justifying this from belief in the incarnation. There, so the argument runs, God demonstrates that he is with us. 'Emmanuel', 'God is with us', is invoked. It follows that the Christian stance with people is also this: to be with them.

BEING WITH: THE SEDUCTION OF 'INCARNATIONAL MINISTRY'

The idea is vague and often produces vacuous, if well-intentioned, behaviour. Asked why he is in a factory, ward or school, or what he is doing on a bereavement visit or at some other moment of pastoral care, the minister replies in such words as, 'In order to be with you.' But that is unsatisfactory. Since it provides no reason why he should be there, this stance does not give people a latching-on point to the pastor and his ministry or message. They then find it difficult either to know what form of association is expected or appropriate, or whether to reject him at any level – friend, counsellor, priest, outsider, insider, and so on. This is not a matter of personality or religious belief. They are unsure with whom they are dealing.

Such ministry is often called 'incarnational'. But it is based upon a deficient grasp of that doctrine. God does not become incarnate in Jesus Christ merely to be at one with humankind. The gospel goes further and addresses the more important issue: 'Why does he do this?' It also speaks of God's achievement and effectiveness – salvation. The Christian calling, therefore, is not merely to be but, by being and believing, to achieve. Without vigilance the pastor and people can slide into a cycle of mutually confirming belief and inaction. The argument runs: 'We are involved in people's lives because they are there; and we are with them as God in Christ is with us.' This sometimes leads to an attitude which demeans others by implying that we understand them. And when that so-called understanding is claimed on the grounds that God was in Christ and therefore he also 'understands', then inadvertent callousness is compounded.

Feelings that are aroused in the pastor are not ends in themselves but tools to be used. They are the main data for the basis on which the minister works. But without interpretation, like all experiences, they are deprived of their impact. All feelings are significant for the pastor, since she works in the arena of people's feelings and experiences. But when she recognizes that people also live at an unconscious level, awareness of the fact and significance of feelings and their need for interpretation becomes even more important. Any pastoral encounter arouses a range of feelings in the minister. They derive from various sources – her own self; the person or group with which she is dealing; the context at large; and, although this is often overlooked, from the fact that minister and people are involved together.

Chaplaincy, such as to schools, industry, commerce or hospitals, is a distinctive instance of incarnational ministry. It is about 'being there', or 'being with', sometimes called 'loitering with intent'. It can easily fall into collusion to justify inaction. We may, however, adopt a proper incarnational stance of being and purpose. When this perspective is taken as the model, although sometimes it may seem that the outcome is odd, nevertheless in that oddity lies potentially the spiritual aspect of people's lives.

Example: an industrial chaplaincy

I was invited to consult to a team of industrial chaplains on the nature of their ministry. They were a team in a major industrial area. It had left its grimy past beind and become a modern business park. The chaplain visited a firm making measuring equipment. He had established a good rapport with staff and workers. He was invited to help outside the factory liturgically – for example, weddings and christenings. He was also asked more frequently than he had expected for advice or comment on religious matters. I studied his ministry and reflected on it in the context provided by every level of the company, from the CEO through to the post boy. I found that the chaplain was welcome and regarded as at least an extension of human resources but indeed a little more. I had a strong sense, however, that I was being given what they believed to be the 'right' answer. The chaplain was helpful, down to earth and someone to whom you could talk. In fact, the company needed him. But when pressed on the 'need' the management and workers alike found it difficult to be precise: he was necessary but it was unclear for what. Eventually at a reflective session after the consultancy had run for some time, as we worked around this issue, one of the junior members of the meeting said, 'The chaplain would be very helpful to us if anybody died.' This was greeted with much serious approval. So I enquired when someone had last died. No one ever had and the prospect of it ever happening seemed remote. This is a clear example of the dependency in which people see their relationship with their minister and, through him or her, God.

But I am sometimes asked whether such an attitude has gone out of date and therefore is not relevant. I can only reply that more recent work on chaplaincy confirms the basic stance: the chaplain (a different one, of course) was still welcome, yet nobody had died at work.

A key instrument in ministry, therefore, is an awareness of these dynamics and sensitivity to the corresponding feelings that are aroused in ministers. The technical term for such feelings is 'counter-transference'. As with transference, its original sense has become more general: as Freud said, 'Everyone possesses in his own unconscious an instrument with which he can interpret the utterances of the unconscious in other people.'[1] If the pastor is to use this facet of her experience, she does not have to ape the therapist. Indeed it is vital that she does not, otherwise she will lose that distinctive point of reference for ministry – the aspects of the incarnation that have formed the basis of this discussion. If she is to be able to use the range of feelings that are aroused in her as she lives and occupies her role as minister with other people, she has to be sufficiently confident of her own identity to be able to face them in herself.

So much is obvious. But this can be taken further. In order to minister to other people she has to recognize that their experience is also unique; that she does not and cannot fully share their feelings. The notion of being one with them is misleading. When, therefore, she feels out of sympathy with another person's predicament, this may be less a sign of failure than a clue to reality and, therefore, of a way into some act of genuine ministry. Awareness of such limitation is the foundation of engagement with others and the essence of pastoral skill in ministry. Anything that blurs this distinction, whether personal anxiety or theological presupposition, hinders ministry on the model of the incarnation.

Here pastoral practice and theological reflection on the incarnation reinforce each other. The various pairs in the doctrine of the incarnation draw our attention to philosophical and theological problems about the nature of God and the person of Jesus Christ. But more importantly they also remind Christians that creative relationships with God and with one another are possible only because of such differences. Religious people expend much effort trying to avoid this. They emphasize unity and oneness, either with God, within God, or with one another. This sounds seductively ideal, not least as a release from fragile human relationships and anxiety about being cut off from the divine source of being. Similarly in pastoral ministry the minister often feels urged towards being at one with everyone – to identify with the poor, the needy, and the casualties of this world. To suggest otherwise seems blasphemous, even though in practice such claimed identity seems to produce impotent responses to people.

The pastor becomes stuck in a bind: she wishes to work effectively with people for God's sake and feels obliged to identify with them; but in so doing she reduces the opportunities for genuinely doing something with them. She assumes that she understands them and so inadvertently slips into a patronizing stance. As a result she may isolate herself more than she knows from those feelings in herself that come from others, which are the key to effective pastoral activity. From the best of intentions and because of an inadequate theological foundation she proves incompetent at the very point where she most wishes to be effective – the pastoral care of people.

ROLES AND PASTORAL MINISTRY

Escape from this impasse lies in holding to two essentials: difference and feeling. One way to do this is to become less aware of the self as person and more alert to role. The model of ministry that Jesus presents confirms this stance. He acknowledged and managed the difference between his person (who he was) and the various roles he was assigned (what people wished him to be). Negotiating this difference within himself, he dealt confidently with people on the basis of those roles, whatever they were. Whether these were defined in relation to God (Messiah), society (teacher, healer) or individuals (carer, brother, friend), they were all used as points on which to build ministry. Similarly, then, on this model ministers are not to strive to be good people who seek to help their neighbours. That may be a pleasant self-image, but it is not useful. The function with roles both in the institutions that sponsor, the churches, and in the fantasies that people hold about them.

In this sense the public minister is not unlike a Messiah. These were the products of traditional Jewish expectation, and specifically of the fantasies that people held about it. Jesus, so far as we can see, did not reject the title (thus accepting a role assigned to him), but avoided endorsing its application to him, most likely for the reason already suggested – the fragile nature of this particular fantasy world. Like him, ministers need to be aware that they are to some extent products of expectations and so be conscious of the wide range of possible, largely fantastic, roles that may be being assigned to them. The pastor can then stay sufficiently in touch with people at a deep level, both so that they can approach him in a way to which he finds himself able to respond and, like Jesus, so as to avoid locking people in fragile worlds of fantasy. This is not an either/or argument. Who they are as persons does matter, but for pastoral ministry in human relationships they need a strong sense of what they are, their role. The emphasis, established for Christians by the model of the incarnation, is always first upon role and second upon person, because in the pastor's assigned roles lies her vulnerability.

Examples: the Good Samaritan and Gethesemane

Two familiar stories from the Gospels illustrate the point. In the parable of the Good Samaritan two characters – a priest and a Levite – have their personal responsibility firmly assigned but then act irresponsibly. The victim makes a demand on them as human beings. This is a continuing point of power in that story, from which no person is exempt. But the critical questions that it poses concern roles: Who is my neighbour? What does it mean in a society to occupy a particular role – that of neighbour to anyone? And, by implication, what does it mean to hold other roles, too, such as priest, Levite or Samaritan? We find a similar emphasis in the account of the agony in Gethsemane. This describes Jesus undergoing personal pain, but the issues raised concern the role of God's servant – what that implies about suffering, and what it means to conform to the requirements of that role in such a way that it does not become an unconstructive constraint on further ministry with people.

The criteria derived from these illustrations of the priority of role also apply in a Christian ministry which is based upon the incarnation and informed by it. It centres on roles and responsibilities: What is it to be a citizen, whether of a nation or of heaven? What is it responsibly to act in particular roles – in the family as father, brother, mother, sister, child, or professionally as manager, producer, salesperson, and so on? The pastor is invited to help to set these and similar issues in a context, since, when she is approached for counsel or pastoring, she is first being addressed in her distinctive role. No doubt in her own mind she is holding a series of roles as confused as those in the minds of the people who come to her. But it is in her assigned role as a representative of the Church or of God that people first approach her, and on this they also found their expectations of her. These may be primitive and magical, but at heart they are religious.

People may consciously approach the minister with an apparently rational understanding of who they are and who she is. But underlying this level of behaviour there are also unconsciously held beliefs and fantasies, which may well not be coherently expressed. Therefore, since anyone working with people now knows that their unconscious mind is as important a factor in their (and her own) life as their conscious behaviour, a way of remaining in touch with this is needed. And because in this encounter roles are of first importance, the source from which the minister derives the criteria to assess her own sense of role (both from within and that assigned by those who approach her) becomes critically important. Furthermore, the minister can see now, from the way that her supreme model of ministry, Jesus Christ incarnate, addresses this dimension of human life, that she cannot and should not minimize or ignore it. She is required to be a religious person, not just a counsellor or befriending human being, and is specifically required to be a Christian minister.

A story of two sisters

This story is taken from the parochial experience of a vicar in an urban parish.

Two sisters shared a house, where they had lived for many years. One was apparently the stronger, taking decisions and generally managing affairs. The other was correspondingly weaker, to the extent of occasionally needing psychiatric treatment. From time to time, however, a reversal took place and the stronger sister became physically ill and appeared in need of support. People believed that the other sister would be unable to cope, and dreaded the future. However, on these occasions the 'weaker' sister blossomed, becoming responsible and managing the affairs of both sisters. Their roles were reversed; the strong became weaker, the weak became stronger.

The vicar of the parish in which they lived had no particular dealings with the sisters. They did not attend his church, but like several people in their area chose to worship in a neighbouring, somewhat older, church. The 'stronger' sister took a leading role there; the 'weaker' had little or no contact. They knew, however, of the vicar of the parish where they lived and he knew about them. One day he was invited to visit the sisters because the 'stronger' had hurt herself and was confined to the house. While he was there the woman who suffered occasional mental disturbance, the so-called 'weaker' one, treated the vicar as more than a casual visitor. She responded to him as someone who represented God. So before he left he deliberately said prayers with them and later took a house communion, mainly for the 'stronger' sister, but with the other also participating. There is still contact between the sisters and the vicar. Sometimes, but by no means regularly, they are seen in his church.

There is, however, a further facet to this story. It appears that many people round about, not only in the immediate environs where the sisters live but also in what might loosely be described as the local community (the vagueness of this term does not matter here), are aware of the sisters and their changed roles. They talk about them and ask the vicar what is happening and how the sisters are getting on, even though they have no personal or direct connection with them. The pair are a focus of some interest on the part of others, who expect the vicar to know about and in a sense to be able to speak for the sisters.

There are many points which could be made, but three illuminate our theme. First, the behaviour of two women, one of whom has a history of psychiatric disturbance, is at first sight not very significant, except to them. People like this are common enough, and on the large scale of human suffering they are of no special consequence. Nevertheless in practice many others are concerned about them. This suggests that some connection is desired and maintained between the comparatively unimportant lives of the pair and the way that others live in the neighbourhood and contribute to local life. In fact more detail on this can be discerned when the area is studied. Their house is at the edge of a part of the town which has a reputation for being depressing and having a large proportion of dependent people. The medical and social services, for example, regard it as an area of heavy demand. In the context of the whole town it is an area which is held in this dependent attitude because it is the receptacle for other areas' projections of incompetence. Yet when examined the estate is shown to produce key leaders in the basic levels of local life – uniformed organizations, charities and other voluntary associations and activities. The lives of these two women – strong and weak, and their reversed roles – seem to match something about the way that the estate and the rest of the town interact.

This observation would not matter greatly in itself, until we note that the local community appears to have no means of expressing itself formally. Because it is held as a place for dependent people, it seems unable to respond. The vicar, however, is allowed to do this. He lives in the area, moves around it, engages with people at basic levels of their lives – birth, marriage and death, as well as in the fundamental associations that make up local life. Even though many have little or nothing to do with his brand of religious belief, his work and the presence of the Church touch the network of life in the area at several points. He is assigned a strange form of authority, to stand for and to affirm that life on that estate does have significance. It is parallel to the woman's assumption that, although she apparently has no intention of joining him in the church, he has authority as God's representative.

THE 'USED' VICAR

The key question, therefore, concerns the vicar's role and usability. His involvement with these two women and the way he is immersed in the life of other groups on the estate, complement each other in assigning him authority to work. And part of that work is to provide a focus where individual life and community living can be interpreted together. He is working in a larger context of ministry and beliefs about the minister than he may immediately be aware. Certainly if he confined his public religious activity to the worship of the Church, his private devotions or his pastoring of the members of the congregation, he would not be able to grasp what was happening to him with individuals and groups in the area. His ministry would, therefore, become increasingly bewildering, until, as frequently happens, he would probably decide to leave.

Second, it is worth noting that the vicar is used also by the sisters to assist them in handling a distinctive dimension of their personal dilemma. They do not need him for therapy or care. Therapy is provided when needed by the psychiatric service, and care in any professional sense is scarcely required. Their relationship dynamically functions to maintain a balance between them, and they are adept at ensuring that their contacts with doctors and others serve their requirements. But one of them, at least, demands that the vicar should explicitly be a religious figure and that he acts in an appropriate manner by praying. If, therefore, he were to ensnare himself in a therapeutic stance alone, he would not be able to engage with the sisters. He might for a time seem to be effective in this one-to-one relationship with them, but this would prove a delusion. They do not need counsel. In addition, his opportunities for working with other groups in the parish would be inhibited. If he becomes too involved with the presenting problems of the sisters, he is less usable in making the interpretative links between their lives and what they represent of the people on the estate as a whole. In order to do anything the vicar has to be first what he is expected to be – a religious figure – and to behave in an appropriate way.

The third point relates to the use made of him in the wider setting of the parish. Through him people believe that they can learn about the sisters. One consequence is that through the notional unit of 'vicar-plus-sisters' they are also able to consider wider issues of their community. It is possible to hear, contrary to every other fantasy, that the estate is not full of dependent depressives, but that inhabitants have not only theoretical authority for their lives but practical ability to do something about it.

Exploration of this would take us too far from our present brief. But we may note the way in which both the sisters and others have expectations of the vicar, especially that in their lives he will 'know what is happening' and will 'understand'. He is not just any figure. His religious function is explicit with the sisters; and others implicitly also use him in this way. The question for him, therefore, is how to minister on more than one front to the sisters and their particular demands, and to the wider area and its less specific, but no less real, needs. One thing is certain: the outcome of such work will not be clear. But that, too, seems to be the character of incarnationally based activity.

We should avoid extravagant claims for such ministry. There are many other points that could be explored in the history of these two women which might, in due course, be useful for ministry. But this story as examined here demonstrates the nature and style of a genuinely incarnational ministry. It is not simply about 'getting alongside' or 'being with' these people, but about being used on several fronts at once. To remain effective there the pastor has to cope with the switching between the roles in which people perceive him. For that the themes of the incarnation are the themes of ministry: boundaries, limitation and negotiation.

BOUNDARIES AS THE KEY

Care about boundaries appears as the minister avoids copying the therapist. He is thrown back repeatedly in this story, whether by the sisters or by other people, on the question of which role is being assigned to him at any moment. It is no use his determining himself as 'priest' or 'minister' or 'Christian'. These are too general. He has to try and discover first which role, however insignificant to him in his self-esteem and self-valuation, is being expected of him. Then he has to test how congruent this is with his public role as Christian minister – and he has to do this quickly on his feet. The idea of boundaries is the key to this stance.

The notion of limitation appears in the nature of the ministry offered. The minister is prepared to be used first rather than to think that he must have some understanding about what is happening before he can intervene. Such ministry is always a problem, since you cannot really know what it involves until you are doing it. But that is precisely the nature of the risk which the model of the incarnation demonstrates.

The minister works consciously in his role, by negotiating between himself and the others. Praying with an emotionally disturbed woman is not the most exciting definition of Christian ministry, especially if the act is isolated and considered apart from everything else. Whatever the theological significance of such prayer, pastoral effectiveness lies not with the woman so much as with the way it establishes the minister's role in his own unconscious mind, so that others can attach their own fantasies to that and so use him in different ways. Thus, because of this fragment of ministry, a range of people, many far removed from the original instance, are enabled better to take up their special roles in the world. This story indicates the central importance of the minister's role, as this is created by negotiation between him and the sisters. Confusion on this point produces some of the strife in contemporary pastoral ministry.

CONCLUSION

The clergy today are sometimes said to have lost their role. As a sociological description this can be discussed, and in those terms there is some evidence in its favour. But there are still public ministers, and people still come to them. The gospel and churches remain. Interactions continue day by day, many of them obvious – as when people meet, talk, help one another – but many of them unconscious. No clear correlation has yet been established between church attendance and Christian influence in an area. All these issues demand the pastor's interpretation.

When loss of role is mentioned, it usually means that pastors have slipped from a self-awareness of their role and of people's expectations of it into a person-based ministry. This inevitably exhausts itself. When such a stance is justified by a naive appeal to an inadequate doctrine of the incarnation as identification, confusion is generated both in ministers and in those who look to them for ministry. Such behaviour is apparently sanctioned by appeal to Christian orthodoxy. We can now see, however, on the theological grounds outlined above and on the basis of the practice of ministry, that incarnation is not about identification but about affirming differences in the series of pairs that it incorporates. It also turns these from being destructive to being creative.

Appreciating limitation, therefore, is one way of discovering identity. Such learning is never an end in itself; it is a form of self-awareness that allows others chance of giving some shape in their minds to what they are approaching. Such ministry is fashioned by the fantasies of others and this world of fantasy can deeply affect them. It disturbs their assumptions about themselves and their roles so that they need assurance that they should be working with such phenomena. The negotiations that this ministry entails are themselves the mark of a creative working relationship from which all involved can discover new things.

It is here, perhaps, that the enigmatic saying of Jesus that anyone who wishes to save his life must lose it (Mark 8.35) takes on new meaning. Purposefully setting the person, with its self-interest and importance, in second place (but not, of course, losing it altogether – otherwise there could be no feelings with which to inform the role), we are more free to uncover and explore the roles that we are being assigned. In that way we find our points of contact with others, most notably with God and our neighbour, and so discover some sort of new life for all.

To make these newly exposed links effective, however, we have to live with them and try to use them. Here the minister is a specific and easily identifiable example of that ministry in which, in various ways, all Christian people play a part. When they confidently take up this type of ministry, they are revitalized as persons or, in traditional Christian language, 'born again' and given new life. This is salvation, and the gospel through which God offers it responds to the most basic parts of ourselves as human beings.

First, it accepts that our anxieties about relationships are well-founded and that they are not merely neurotic symptoms. Relationships of every sort are fragile, involving, as they do, the problems of limitation and negotiation. Second, however, it declares that these dynamics are not restrictions on our lives, since God himself has affirmed them in the person of Jesus Christ as his own way of being. Here grace abounds: no human being has first to change or deny their basic humanity, including its unconscious aspects, in order to encounter God. Third, conversion comes about when these fundamental aspects of ourselves are transformed. Because God through the incarnation addresses us in our unconscious, our relationships are perceived as possessing increased richness and significance. They cease to be foci for mere hopefulness and ultimately for disappointment. Instead they become genuine bearers of realistic hope. Differences between people, the felt gap between God and humankind, and the divisions inside each of us, are not hindrances to life.

Finally, therefore, believers are invited both by God and by their neighbours to accept without being distressed the often strange roles which people assign to them. The pastor uses his feelings to interpret these expectations for the benefit of others and not for himself. The minister in particular may have to accept the awesome role of 'God-person', with its overtones of magic, fear and avoidance, just as Jesus had to accept, but not endorse, the unsuitable role of Messiah in order to be usable as the Son of Man. It may even, therefore, be that the pastor's role should be sustained as qualitatively different from that of the laity, in spite of contemporary pressure to minimize any such distinction. With their fear of difference, limitation and negotiation, church people may too casually leap to conclusions about all Christians being one, without reflecting on what any differences may signify in terms of usability. The incarnation provides a consistently demanding model of how, even in the most sensitive parts of his ministry, the pastor's role is the critical agent. Those who remain faithful to this role are crucified. Persons merely die. The difference, if the minister is not to delude himself and others, is vital.

CHAPTER ELEVEN

Only by prayer: incarnation and the disciples' prayer

Each of the fundamental doctrines that we are examining is also grounded in Christian discipleship. Whatever the contemporary skills they may deploy, pastors cannot afford to lose sight of their distinctively Christian vocation. This is founded upon faith and practice – in a word, discipleship. Until recently this might have been stated without argument. But in line with the contemporary assumption that leadership is everything, churches themselves have been preoccupied with this theme. Many have assumed a model of ministerial leadership that they believe will build up a congregation.

It is therefore all the more apposite that the pastor's vocation should continue to be seen in terms of discipleship. The religious practice to which the incarnation relates is prayer. For the key issue which any religious body must ultimately address is how people can be in touch with God.

DISCIPLESHIP AND PRAYER

There are so many books, courses and teaching programmes on prayer that we might think prayer is the prerogative of religious people. But that would be to start at the wrong point. We are not first thinking of spiritual achievements in prayer, but of the widespread religious phenomenon of prayer through which people attempt to or believe that they contact God. On this issue contemporary Christians sometimes find themselves out of tune with common human experience. Prayer is one of the most prevalent human activities, yet in the life of the Church it seems increasingly a problem. Most believers consider prayer part of their everyday routine, but many regard it as not very useful for achieving practical effect. On the one hand what would it be to be

Christian and not pray? Praying is a minimum qualification for being Christian. Meetings often begin with the ritual, whether the prayer is perfunctory or fervently extempore. Yet on the other hand praying seems futile. Some claim that prayer is vital and testably influential, but most believers live with uneasy feelings of irrelevance and ineffectiveness. What, for example, do our persistent prayers for social justice or political change achieve? And what of the many prayers for implied personal benefit or advantage? These are public. Who knows what is said in private? Prayer as Christian practice is ambiguous. It is a central dimension of Christian behaviour which nevertheless pushes us to the margins of our faith. Ostensibly looking to God in confidence, we find our reflective selves doubting.

Yet this Christian practice harnesses a major area of common human experience and the Christian doctrine of the incarnation. 'O God!' or 'Jesus!', as exclamations of exasperation, may not sound much like prayers. Yet in a crude fashion they are. No rational thought is given to whom they are addressed, but that is rarely the case with any instinctive cry. Somewhere underlying this casualness may still lie a sense of someone or something other than the self with whom a needed link is being made. More refined prayers are consciously said, even by those who claim no allegiance to any church. This is a seldom examined example of religious dependence.

PRAYER, A UNIVERSAL PHENOMENON

In a study refining general sociological surveys of implicit, common or folk religion, by addressing his questions to claimed experience rather than to publicly observable activity, David Hay was confronted, as he put it, with a series of puzzles. For example, at a time when in much of mainland Europe and the UK church membership and attendance is statistically lower, why do religious activities like prayer remain so prevalent? But prayer expresses expectation. We resort to it when things are, or seem to be, beyond control. Caught between events which feel unmanageable and the need to take decisions, we articulate as an interim measure our hope that by making a connection with the Almighty (otherwise disregarded, possibly not believed in, and certainly given little attention as a realistic resolver of problems) the issue might be better handled. This is not an expressed intention to do something. It is an ejaculated expectation that we already know is unlikely to be realized. No one would be more surprised at an obviously divine intervention than the person praying. Prayer as a religious phenomenon is an instance of hopefulness created by making a connection between the praying person and some notion of God.

THE DISCIPLES' PRAYING

The Christian disciple at prayer, however, claims to be engaged in more than this, and history provides numerous instances of individuals and, through their liturgies, of churches which have refined this practice. This spiritual activity may not be in itself distinctive; it is rooted in common human experience. Its focus, however, is different. For the Christian Church, prayer is primarily a means by which Christians become increasingly competent in their roles. But before going further we should now define the range covered by the word 'prayer'.

People sometimes wish to turn all normal activities into prayer. But such generalizations are not very helpful. If every activity is prayer, what precisely is it to pray? Neither can we transform prayer into action; activity itself then merely replaces prayer. The general term 'spirituality' is frequently used to disguise this confusion. That notion stands for the general style of Christian living and we shall study this later. Today in our liturgically preoccupied churches we risk confining the idea of prayer to public liturgy and make it part of shared experience. There is a connection between liturgy and praying, but to transform all prayer into a liturgical act also diminishes it.

Prayer, as understood in common human experience, takes a specific form. It is deliberate (litugical ordering has much influence on personal prayer); intimate (the language is often erotic); and personally questioning (the desires of the person praying often come back to make demands on them). Here we are dealing in prayer as a conscious, personal directing of the self towards God. Once that position is reached, prayer seems to be not unlike transference. The person praying puts herself in the way of memory as well as desire. That is why prayer so often takes the form of the indicative – statements of 'fact', though more usually of belief. This may include telling the Almighty something about himself: the opening of prayers that begin 'O God, you are etc. . . . '. This is frequently followed by the optative – 'Would that you would . . .' – expressing what the person praying would wish to receive whether for themselves or for others. Unlike therapy, in which patient and therapist forge an intense dyad, any and every public role of the Christian exposes an underlying triad – God, neighbour, the person praying.

From this persepective we may discern two major types of prayer. The first is comprised of meditation and contemplation. How is our joining with God established? On what sort of basis could a relationship be developed? Spiritual directors some-times distinguish the two types, but they are always closely connected. We might think of meditation as concerned with our partnership with God. Contemplation then has to do with our own self-awareness. The second form of prayer is intercession, prayer offered for others.

MEDITATION

Meditation in Christian practice is different from those forms of meditating that are urged, for example, upon harassed business-men. They are encouraged to create restful space within the maelstrom of stress. That space is itself the focus of the medita-tion, although an object such as a vase of flowers or a statue may be provided to help. Christian meditation, however, is specifically directed to the life, ministry, death and resurrection of Jesus Christ. This is not merely observed or adored. Meditation requires participation. Meditating on the story of Jesus, we become intensely aware of these boundaries between ourselves and God and between ourselves and our neighbours and within our own selves. As we focus outside ourselves on the person of Jesus Christ, we are pressed to try and get straight this series of relations, both outside and within.

These are exactly the connections which are fundamental in the incarnation and to any sound practice of pastoral ministry. Prayer as meditation, therefore, is not primarily concerned with who is the subject and who the object in the dialogue between myself and God, but with the process itself. When we meditate on the incarnate Christ, we may hope to become like him. Such hopes are not wishes. There are as many Jesuses as there are fan-tasies that we can have about ourselves – gentle and considerate, a powerful teacher, an exorcist, the confronter of tyrants or scourge of religiosity. These may confirm the beliefs that some people hold, but they render the Christian faith vulnerable to psychological criticism. The result of this is that the Christian life becomes more problematical for many believers and, more importantly, for those with whom we wish to share the interpretative stance derived from our faith.

To become like Christ is not to become like our own (or for that matter like any other) image of him, but to take into ourselves through prayer and practice the distinctive model of the incarnation. This is not 'Jesus', but is the series of processes that we have discerned in our earlier discussion. It demonstrates that creative living is possible when we affirm limitations and risk negotiations on this basis. Through meditation we can better discern critical boundaries, chiefly through becoming increasingly alive to the major boundary between our self and God.

We are now speaking of God and the human soul. 'Soul' has largely fallen into disuse. But the word still has a distinctive and valuable use. It describes the human person viewed as the image of God. Negotiation between God and man, establishing the boundaries of the self and of God through meditation, is crucial for the survival of this dimension of our humanity.

Confronted by various assaults upon religion, belief and the Church, Christians have to a degree withdrawn from this field. As a result we have become impervious to the questions being directed at our belief by the various social sciences and, more significantly, by ordinary people whose lives have been informed by them. Christians have responded in terms of religion's personal and social usefulness. But the point of contact and thus of mutual illumination between Christian doctrine, common human experience and religious behaviour will not be in shared action alone. It will involve holding to the apparent uselessness, but essential need for all humanity, of prayer. If, however, Christians do not sustain the model of the incarnation as the linking paradigm, they will lose the focus for their meditation and hence for their distinctive life. They will then be unable to take the opportunities which arise for interpretation of and contribution to the life of others. For even this most intimate or private religious activity carries implications for others.

The recovery of the soul may be one thing that is vitally needed today to preserve the human race. That is not the judgement of a Christian alone. Others, too, as they observe the responses that we humans make to the pressures of living in mass societies, have issued the same challenge. Prayer as meditation on the model of the incarnation, therefore, is nothing less than a key means to human salvation.

CONTEMPLATION

Meditation focuses outwards from the self to Jesus Christ. Contemplation looks within, so that, as we pray, we become more aware of ourselves. An occasional outcome is the ecstatic wish to lose oneself and to be absorbed in Christ, which has been regarded as the height of spiritual experience. But, as we have already noted, this is inadequate as a proclamation of the Christian life. What is more, it offers no point of engagement with contemporary spiritualities. These have a quality of contemplation about them, as people seek ways of affirming a personal dimension to human life – meaning, value and purpose.

In the context of that search, talk of the loss of self is incomprehensible. As the feeling and thinking agent, the self is central to the agenda and cannot be relegated to the periphery. There is little point in trying to interpret all human experience in the light of the gospel unless we are prepared to value that experience in its own right. In addition, the notion of loss of self does not accurately represent Christian contemplation. It carries overtones of merging, so that, if self-awareness is removed, somehow there is no obstacle to everything being seen as 'God'. If one term in the encounter is absorbed into the other, then there can be no meeting. In an age when one of the searches is for personal significance and identity, it is no gospel to begin by implying that you have to lose what you seek before you have found it and had a chance to explore it. The other side of this, which appears from time to time in the Christian tradition, is that God ceases to be needed as God, since the sum of spirituality is all self. The sublime moment of true insight is claimed to occur when we abandon God. But this approach, too, fails to engage with common human experience or with the religious experience of most. To take leave of God represents a sophistication which remains beyond the capacity of most, and is therefore doubtful as a normative experience of the religious life. The persistence of religion, too, runs counter to this trend. It still tends to add encrustation around prevailing ideas of God in some form, and shows little sign of declining. There is a theological significance to this, which cannot be ignored.

Meditation alerts us to boundaries; contemplation to negotiation. In thinking about the incarnation, we saw that a series of linkings was needed to sustain the world in hope. But the profound experience which follows, when we come to see and value such connections, is one of extraordinary vulnerability. This appears wherever we turn in our reflection on these linkings. Divine vulnerability begins to emerge in the incarnation, as God opens himself to scrutiny. Our vulnerability is similar, when we reflect on how fragile our relations are with one another and with God. Vulnerability is not a quality added to these relations; it is intrinsic as the result of the effort that is needed to preserve their tensions and to keep them creative.

Contemplation, therefore, has a specific function. It is a consciously self-reflective act, practised in order to maintain the tension and vulnerability of that incarnation which is the object of meditation and the model of ministry. It is, therefore, stressful work, calling for an intellectual and emotional integrity, which is easy to think about but demanding to exercise. It is also difficult because it depends upon meditation, our focusing on the model of God's activity which is made known in Jesus. In the new context created by that prayer, Christian contemplation follows as we enter upon self-reflection, which neither denies our selves nor merely affirms them. By this means the model of the incarnation is so absorbed that it instinctively becomes the reflective stance for pastoral ministry.

Meditation and contemplation in the light of our thinking about the incarnation give the command to watch and pray (Matthew 26.41) renewed meaning. To watch is to hold the processes of the incarnation as the focus of our meditation; to pray is to sustain that model in ourselves through that contemplation in which we repeatedly negotiate between ourselves and Christ. As Christians, we pray by meditating on the limitations of our lives and their usability and by exploring various boundaries as they emerge in our dealings with ourselves and God.

INTERCESSION

Meditation and contemplation establish the Christian's role; intercession is about making that role work. This is also another fraught area. Whether it be to save the starving in Africa by praying for rain, or the profits of the village fête by praying for sun, the exercise is incredible. But the expressions of hope in each case are not meaningless. The dynamic that we perceive in the incarnation illuminates intercession and connects it with both faith and pastoral practice, whatever the persisting philosophical problems.

At the heart of the matter lies the difference between hope and hopefulness. It is today a commonplace to think of God as the end towards which all things tend. But theologies of hope are often difficult to grasp, since we do not easily distinguish general feelings of optimism or hopefulness from genuine hope – that life-sustaining stance which is engendered less from within than through effective negotiation between ourselves and our context.

Hope is the crucial issue in intercession. Through such prayer we discover again that the conscious and unconscious dynamics of our human life in relationships are not merely a given context for living. We are to understand them as an aspect of his creation with which God has deliberately engaged. Once we see that, we have a ground for working on the difference between genuine hope and fantasized hopefulness.

The two are separable, but in the muddiness of human life we frequently confuse them. The tendency to idealize, which runs through our unconscious life, leads to optimism which is un-related to reality. This sometimes emerges in religion as inter-cessory prayer. But if we grasp that those aspects of ourselves which produce this result can be employed for mature living, then no prayer need become mere hopefulness or fantasy. The means by which we can discern what is happening is offered by the model of the incarnation.

In intercessory praying we consciously take back into ourselves what we are part of – those relationships with God, our neigh-bour and ourselves that we are invited by the model of the incar-nation to interpret through God's involvement in such pairs. To pray in this way sets us firmly in our role as people of God within its context of the wider world. This ceases to be populated by me and my fantasies alone – although they will be there and will be tested by the exercise. The world's realities are introduced into worship and prayer exactly at the point where we are most acutely aware of our role in relation to God. We have to articulate them, not as if we are reading the news to God, but in the con-fused and emotionally laden state that we are in. In intercession world issues are not outside us; they are offered as they are found inside us, whether directly, because we are immediately caught up in them, or distantly, because we are partially aware of them and their seriousness.

We cannot, therefore, intercede without evaluating our motives. But we are now, because of our reflection on the incarna-tion, aware that prayer on behalf of others will involve us in questioning who these others are and what they represent to and for us. They cannot be offered to God by us without our also offering our own participation, in whatever form that takes. It might be thought, however, that such a view of intercession implies that the only change that may come about is in our perspective on ourselves. One result certainly is heightened awareness of our roles and responsibilities in the world. But such self-awareness does not benefit us alone; intercessory prayer, when seen in this light, is also a significant contribution to the well-being of others and of the world in general. For it offers a means by which altruism can be affirmed and activated.

One disabling effect of contemporary scepticism is that any altruistic stance is automatically suspect. Some argue on the basis of biology or psychology that genuine altruism is inconceivable. Self-interest will always dominate. But even if this is true in a clinical sense (and that is arguable), in common human experience altruism is necessary if people are not to degenerate into a series of self-enclosed, private and other-disregarding individuals or groups. In intercessory prayer we address in a practical way this universal question: Can one person act on behalf of another for that person's benefit and well-being? Pastoral practice, the model of the incarnation and the distinctively religious activity of prayer coincide and mutually inform each other around this question and demand a confident, but realistically based, affirmative answer.

This heightened awareness of others demonstrates the significance of intercession in the context of human relations and the incarnation. Pairing represents a primitive aspect of our unconscious selves. It seems to be a means by which we deal with a rage which may either destroy ourselves and others or be harnessed to creative partnership. This unconscious process, the detail of which does not matter here, explains many of those ambivalent feelings which we frequently experience at intercession. On the one hand we think that it is a good thing to pray for others and praying, therefore, earns us kudos. Yet on the other hand, when we think objectively about it, it seems a foolish and apparently useless thing to do, and it can stimulate unadmitted anger against those who seek, or even seem to demand, our prayers.

This is one reason why there is so much unhelpful intercession in the Church's public worship. This prayer is often used by congregations and ministers alike as a way of defending themselves against their feelings of impotent anger at God for the way the world is. Because ministers and congregations are uncertain about intercession, it becomes the part of the service that anyone is allowed to do. It is divorced from the structure and detail of the worship and from the concerns which the congregation as a whole may have. An individual is left to manage this problematic piece of religious activity. And, when their attempt proves irrelevant or unhelpful, it is easier to castigate the leader, publicly or privately, than to acknowledge our own rage against a God who allows the world to be as it is and himself to be so impotent, when he is – so we at least unconsciously assume – being sustained by our worship.

The content of prayers also demonstrates this underlying wish to protect ourselves from our feelings about God. This often degenerates into self-affirming thanksgiving, stressing God's blessings to his people, and by implication disposing of others as the unblessed. At other times it becomes thinly disguised exhortation. Because it is difficult, intercession often ceases to be prayer offered to God on behalf of all others, and degenerates into self-congratulation. It is probable, therefore, that Jesus' story about the Pharisee and the publican (Luke 18.10–14) was about intercession. If, however, we can integrate this basic Christian activity with our pastoral practice and theological perception, we can face this tendency to defend ourselves and the feelings which are associated with it. By so doing we can also be enabled to move away from exclusive attitudes, which produce destructive behaviour, and begin to look at the world and ourselves in terms of co-operative, creative activity with God and with one another.

CHAPTER TWELVE

Conclusion

CHRISTIANITY AND THE HUMAN SCIENCES

No long conclusion is needed: the pastoral theologian's context is ministering. The pastor can only be the theologian in so far as he is about his normal business. That is where his contribution originates. The argument here has been that the Church at this moment in its history has to think through its basic doctrines once more. To do this it needs to take into greater account the human sciences. This will both assist pastors in communicating with others and enable them better to integrate doctrine, pastoral activity and their own spirituality. Because the pastor deals with groups (even the single penitent is representing others), we also need some understanding both of groups and of the individual that is coherent. We cannot perpetually think solely in terms of the individual. Here such an approach is offered and applied. Not surprisingly the basic underlying human dynamics emerge in three primary doctrines of the faith – atonement, resurrection and incarnation.

There is a history of suspicion about the behavioural sciences on the part of Christians, but there is no need for it. The common interest and focus is humankind, which is fundamental to the faith of the pastor and basic to others involved with the human sciences. The fact that they may not say much about God is, at least in part, met by the common acknowledgement of transcendence. This may be personalized as 'almighty God' or more impersonally as 'the task' – the overarching reason for a programme or enterprise.

The implication [of the ease with which the word 'God' is used] might seem to be that Christians have no difficulty today about the reality of God in the world as we have it today; that the world does not believe in that reality, but the Church does, and all that is necessary is to find the right words, the proper conviction and correct apologetic . . . Things are not quite as simple as that, and the problem concerns belief in God within the Church and not only outside it. The fact is that some, I do not say many, and certainly not most, but some convinced Christians do not find it at all easy either to grasp or to communicate the reality of God in today's society.[1]

MINISTRY LAY AND ORDAINED

It may also seem that the ministry described here is excessively clerical: it concerns the work done by some sort of publicly authorized person. This focal point still distresses some people. After all, we live in a Church in which after the century of the laity (the twentieth century) we are still not clear about the distinction between orders and the relatedness of clergy and lay people. Sometimes distinctions are obliterated by reference to 'all baptized' or 'every member ministry'. But it does not follow from that usually egalitarian approach that there is no hierarchy of relationships. Indeed we have seen that, if we are to engage with people in any sort of dependent mode, they need a sensed hierarchy. It is noticeable in the New Testament, for instance, that in some fashion all may have a ministry. But it is not recognized as so significant inside the Church. The criteria for the selection of leaders are not even specifically Christian. They are mostly everyday virtues that link them with other civilized citizens.[2] The Pastoral Epistles, regardless of their date and authorship, reinforce that view, and that gives us a clue to the nature of ministry. It is a negotiated concept, determined by those outside the Church with those within. This is, of course, unconscious behaviour, but there seems to be a link. The chapters on the three major theological topics seek, like the pastor, to sustain this stance.

PASTORAL STUDIES

What of pastoral studies? If we recognize that these are theologically founded and psychologically sound, we need a way of holding these aspects together without imposing them on others or on ourselves. The Church is always fascinated by integration, its own unity being a critical issue from the first. Here we elaborated two aspects of necessary coherence. One is the link between role and ministry; the other concerns the pastor's personal faith and the public expectation. This latter seems to persist even though public association with the Church remains low.

A DECLINING CHURCH?

There can be scarcely anyone in the Church who does not regret the decline in congregations. Once we have run through 'believing without belonging' (Davie) and 'the myth of the empty church' (Gill) and other psychological and sociological pieces, the fact remains that the growing population – discounting other faiths – is not being matched by growing congregations and churches. That is the prevailing picture. In practice, however, as I, until recently, moved around the Church of England (I cannot speak for other Churches), I found there are signs that those who work in it faithfully are those who most often find people looking for association with the Church.

SIGNS OF HOPE

Three stories come to mind. The first is a team parish in the rough end of a northern city. Here a group of six men and women minister in this deprived area of their own volition. They are pulling together to make the Church's presence (there are six parishes) more free in that society and not so hidebound by its buildings and other constraints. The team is not united: they disagree. But as a team it coalesces around major pieces of work. For the moment part of their work is to find out what the future picture of the Church in that environment should be. They grasp something of the projections and dependence in that area. These dynamics they accept with some understanding. And they have seen congregations grow, in one case from three to thirty – an extraordinary percentage. There is no sign of any wish to leave or give up: there is every sign of enthusiasm for this ministry.

The second theme is cathedrals and greater churches. In many cases large numbers of people come. This is not just for visiting but for private prayer and to affirm aspects of their society, to remember the past and pray for the present and future. The cathedrals are very busy with demands made upon them. For to find anonymity in order to seek God requires a large setting in which to hide. Our stripped-down local churches cannot offer this. Cathedral and local church are not in competition. This is something to cherish.

The third and last point comes from a bishop's staff meeting. It is not a scientific study but it represents something that formal figures do not – and cannot – show. The bishop and his senior colleagues were considering the church statistics and could not disagree with them. But at the same time they felt more in touch than the figures seemed to show. The bishop did a rough count and reckoned that in the course of the year something like 51 per cent of the population (not church people) had some dealings with the church – a wedding or funeral, school events, and an encounter with the pastor for some reason. Probably this is a high percentage compared with some other parts of Great Britain, but nevertheless it is a significant figure. Even when allowance is made for the clerical predisposition to exaggerate, all this gives some indication of what people are looking for from the Church in the present century. The dynamic key to this lies in the basic assumptions – particularly dependency, with its wish for simple solutions to complex issues to be energized, but not by me or this group.

POLITICAL AND SOCIAL PASTORING

One major development in pastoral studies has been a turning away from a preoccupation with the individual and a closer look at the setting in which pastoral care occurs. Issues such as justice, care for the poor, women's rights and other liberation causes begin to find a home under the banner of 'pastoral'. Why do we assume that pastoral study and care for those in distress should be confined to the individual? The social context is vital.

Example: William Booth

When in the late nineteenth century William Booth established his mission in the East End of London, he realized that many of the problems facing the distressed poor were due to alcohol. It was the day of the slogan 'drunk for a penny, dead drunk for tuppence'. His Protestant zeal for saving souls made the assumption that the individual alone mattered. It was, however, not long before he realized that he had to work for social change so that the context in which individuals were brought up could be more conducive to generating responsibility. He also saw the foolishness of bringing a drunk off the street and then at their first act of worship, the holy communion, to pour wine down their throats. So a non-Eucharistic church was instituted.

Almost two decades have passed since the first edition of this book. I naively thought that a modest revision could be easily done. But it was not so. A major rewrite has been required. Pastoral studies as a discipline have developed; theological reflection is being required of all engaged in ministry. I am struck, however, when talking with clergy, that there seems to be no shortage of pastoral opportunities. But sometimes the Church seems to abandon them too easily because of its own discomfort or ministerial dogma. It is easier to locate blame in the people, not in the Church. How many sermons do we hear berating those who have not attended – 'those outside'?

In another dimension of church life in England – the establishment – the same applies. Adrian Hastings, who resisted the establishment for much of his life, came to realize that to be faithful today Christians have no choice but to sustain *every* opportunity for encounter, whatever the cost.[3]

Contemporary ministry requires pastors who can minister with people at present outside or on the margins of the Church. This will not only serve people, it will also benefit the Church:

> The protection against doctrine becoming ossified or defensively conservative lies in the extent to which the church adheres to its distinctive task. For if it does this, it will find itself permanently caught up in practical tussles which heightens the critical question of why a particular point of belief matters.[4]

The task referred to is that of taking the confused feelings in any situation, discerning as best one may the prevailing dynamic and then interpreting for the benefit of others, but with a profound reflexive effect on the Church, too. Formation for that ministry requires the integration of activity, theology and discipleship. All three are needed. For such a ministry will continually stress the minister at the point where his or her personal faith and public role intersect. It will also clarify roles, thus making more effective the interchange with others. But all this is done because the pastor is Christian, not in spite of that. Therefore, ministry must creatively interact with the Church's developing theology, making a distinctive contribution.

To achieve that we require a unifying theme. That which links the individual to his or her social context and hence to society is found in the contemporary human sciences. The inspiration of ministry, the clarification of roles and theological reflection potentially hold the whole enterprise together. Difficult and strange as that often appears, it still seems to me to remain intrinsically worthwhile.

Notes

PREFACE

1 E. Graham, H. Walton and F. Ward (2006), *Theological Reflection: Methods*, London: SCM Press.
2 P. Hebblethwaite (1978), *The Year of the Three Popes*, London: Collins.

1 INTRODUCTION

1 E. J. Miller and A. K. Rice (1967), *Systems of Organisation*, London: Tavistock, p. 17.
2 H. Meng and E. L. Freud, eds (1963), *Psychoanalysis: The Letters of Sigmund Freud and Oskar Pfister*, New York: Basic Books.
3 C. Rycroft (1985), *Psychoanalysis and Beyond*, London: Chatto & Windus, p. 26.
4 The bishop said that the resurrection was 'not a conjuring trick with bones', but was always misquoted without the 'not'.
5 S. Freud, 'An autobiographical study', in *The Standard Edition of the Complete Psychological Works*, vol. 20.
6 E. R. Shapiro and A. W. Carr (1991), *Lost in Familiar Places*, New Haven: Yale University Press.

2 THE ATONEMENT: FOR US AND FOR OUR SALVATION

1 M. F. Wiles (1982), *Faith and the Mystery of God*, London: SCM Press, p. 53.
2 This is Moltmann's 'text' – see below, p. 24.
3 For more on these forms of prayer, see below, pp. 157–66.
4 George Cavafy, 'Waiting for the barbarians'. There are several versions.
5 W. Pannenberg (1968), *Jesus, God and Man*, ET London: SPCK, p. 268.
6 It seems to me that there is such a difference in nuance. But see for another opinion, C. F. D. Moule, *An Idiom Book of New Testament Greek*, Cambridge: Cambridge University Press.

3 WORKING VULNERABILITY:
THE ATONEMENT AND PASTORAL CARE

1 E. Schweizer (1971), *Jesus*, ET London: SCM Press, p. 45.
2 The word 'priest' is deliberately used here, because formally confession and absolution have been part of the priest's function. However, readers who do not hold this view of ministry will be able to substitute their own description of this minister and whatever setting would for them replace the confessional.
3 G. Fourez (1983), *Sacraments and Passages*, Notre Dame: Ave Maria Press, p. 130.
4 J. N. D. Kelly (1972), *Early Christian Creeds*, London: A & C Black, p. 151.
5 The first unequivocal use of the word 'martyr' to designate one who witnesses and dies is in connection with Polycarp, who died in Smyrna in 155 CE (*Martyrdom of Polycarp* 19.1), but the link between witness and death goes back to Stephen (Acts 22.20), and (implicitly) to Jesus' crucifixion (Revelation 1.5).

4 TAKING UP YOUR CROSS:
ATONEMENT AND THE DISCIPLES' SPIRITUALITY

1 Lutheran apophthegm.

5 GOD SAW THAT IT WAS GOOD:
THE DOCTRINE OF CREATION

1 J. Moltmann (1979), *The Crucified God*, ET London: SCM Press, p. 120.

6 ON THE THIRD DAY HE ROSE AGAIN:
THE DOCTRINE OF THE RESURRECTION

1 G. Wainwright (1980), *Doxology: A Systematic Theology*, London: Epworth, p. 26.
2 S. Millar (1968), *The Psychology of Play*, Harmondsworth: Penguin, p. 255.
3 There are several terms, each slightly nuanced – folk, residual, customary, common religion – and more.

8 ENJOYING GOD:
CREATION, RESURRECTION AND THE DISCIPLES' WORSHIP

1 This is not the same as Bruce Reed's oscillation theory, although there are similarities. See B. D. Reed (1978), *The Dynamics of Religion*, London: Darton, Longman & Todd.
2 See Northrop Frye (2003), 'Conclusion to the second edition of *Literary History of Canada*', in *Northrop Frye on Canada*, ed. J. O'Grady and D. Staines, Toronto and London: University of Toronto Press, p. 464.
3 This should be taken carefully since societies change. The aristocracy, for example, have perhaps been superseded by 'celebrities'.

9 AND BECAME MAN:
INCARNATION, LIMITATION AND NEGOTIATION

1 M. F. Wiles (1976), *Working Papers on Doctrine*, London: SCM Press, p. 102.
2 The title 'Christian' was assigned not assumed. The people of Antioch recognized them.
3 'Kenotic' (from the Greek *kenosis*, meaning 'emptying') describes theories of the incarnation which, based on Philippians 2.7, emphasize the self-limitation of the divine attributes of the Son of God.
4 The distinction between 'delusion' and 'illusion' is especially important in this context. Delusion means the loss of contact with reality and is a pathological state; 'illusion' refers to our attempts to find meaning in experience and wishes, which is the way in which we construct realities, a normal life process.

10 GOD IS WITH US:
INCARNATION AND PASTORAL CARE

1 S. Freud, 'The disposition to obsessional neurosis', *The Standard Edition of the Complete Psychological Works*, vol. 12, p. 314.

12 CONCLUSION

1 T. G. A. Baker (1983), Speech to General Synod.
2 In Timothy 3.7, for example, the bishops should manifest sound citizenship in the world outside as much as they are supposed to order the Church inside. This stance towards the non-Christian world in which the Church emerged is confirmed by the use of the 'house tables' in the epistles (Colossians 3.18ff. and 1 Peter 3.1ff.). These were, of course, 'Christianized' as now being 'in Christ'.
3 A. Hastings (1986), *A History of English Christianity, 1920 to 1985*, London: Collins.
4 A. W. Carr (1983), 'A teaching church with a collective mind', *Crucible*, a paper for the Canterbury Convocation on its seven-hundredth anniversary.

Further reading

This is not any sense a bibliography of pastoral studies, but a number of books which could assist in further study. As will be realized, the range of disciplines is considerable.

The New Dictionary of Pastoral Studies (SPCK, 2002) would be a useful book to have at hand. It is designed to assist readers when they encounter unfamiliar concepts or technical terms.

PASTORAL STUDIES

[These authors address key questions from a variety of perspectives, to which the titles draw attention.]

P. H. Ballard (1986), *The Foundations of Pastoral Studies and Practical Theology*, Cardiff: University College.

P. H. Ballard and J. Pritchard (2006), *Practical Theology in Action*, 2nd edn, London: SPCK.

A. B. Campbell (1985), *Paid to Care? The Limits of Professionalism in Pastoral Care*, London: SPCK.

A. W. Carr (1994), *Brief Encounters: Pastoral Ministry Through Baptisms, Weddings and Funerals*, London: SPCK.

A. W. Carr (1997), *Handbook of Pastoral Studies*, London: SPCK.

E. Graham, H. Walton and F. Ward (2005), *Theological Reflection: Methods*, London: SCM Press.

S. Pattison (1988), *A Critique of Pastoral Care*, London: SCM Press.

S. Pattison (1994), *Pastoral Care and Liberation Theology*, Cambridge: Cambridge University Press.

HISTORY

W. A. Clebsch and C. R. Jaekle (1975), *Pastoral Care in Historical Perspective*, New York: Aronson.

G. R. Evans (ed.) (2000), *A History of Pastoral Care*, London: Cassell. *[This recent collection covers the whole field.]*

BACKGROUNDS

[Two seminal books relating theology to the human sciences.]

J. Bowker (1973), *The Sense of God: Sociological, Anthropological and Psychological Approaches to the Origin of the Sense of God*, Oxford: Clarendon.

J. Bowker (1978), *The Religious Imagination and the Sense of God*, Oxford: Oxford University Press.

[Freud's extensive writings are collected in a Standard Edition.]

S. Freud (1900), *The Interpretation of Dreams*.

S. Freud (1925), *An Autobiographical Study*.

S. Freud (1927), *The Future of an Illusion*.

S. Freud (1930), *Civilisation and its Discontents*.

S. Freud (1939), *Moses and Monotheism*.

S. Freud and O. Pfister (1963), *Psychoanalysis and Faith*, New York: Basic Books.

O. Pfister (1928), *The Illusion of the Future*, ET, H. Meng and E. L. Freud (1963), *Psychoanalysis and Faith: The Letters of Sigmund Freud and Oskar Pfister*, New York: Basic Books.

HUMAN SCIENCES AND ALLIED MATERIAL

Sociological and similar studies

G. Davie (1994), *Religion in Britain since 1945: Believing Without Belonging*, Oxford: Blackwell.

R. Gill (1975), *The Social Context of Theology*, London: Mowbrays.

R. Gill (1993), *The Myth of the Empty Church*, London: SPCK.

D. Hay (1987), *Exploring Inner Space*, Oxford: Mowbrays.

Systems and organization

E. J. Miller (1993), *From Dependency to Autonomy: Studies in Organisation and Change*, London: Free Association.

E. J. Miller and A. K. Rice (1967), *Systems of Organisation*, London: Tavistock.

The psychoanalytically informed perspective

W. R. Bion (1961), *Experiences in Groups and Other Papers*, London: Tavistock

W. W. Meissner (1984), *Psychoanalysis and Religious Experience*, New Haven: Yale University Press.

M. Pines (ed.) (1985), *Bion and Group Psychotherapy*, London: Routledge and Kegan Paul. *[This book is badly titled. It includes valuable essays that go far beyond psychotherapy.]*

B. D. Reed (1978), *The Dynamics of Religion*, London: Darton, Longman & Todd.

E. R. Shapiro and A. W. Carr (1991), *Lost in Familiar Places: Making New Connections between the Individual and Society*, New Haven: Yale University Press.

Index